Minnesota Underfoot

*A Field Guide
to the State's Outstanding
Geologic Features*

WRITTEN BY
Constance J. Sansome
PHOTOGRAPHS BY
Kenneth N. Sansome
ILLUSTRATIONS BY
James E. Kiehne

VOYAGEUR PRESS • 1983

Acknowledgments

I give profound thanks to the Minnesota Natural Heritage Program and Barbara Coffin, the Minnesota Geological Survey, and especially John Splettsstoesser. These organizations and individuals have aided me in the research for and preparation of this manuscript. I thank Dr. H. E. Wright, Jr., limnologist and geologist at the University of Minnesota, for deepening my knowledge of and respect for the land, George Gambsky and Bonnie Connor at the Art Center of Minnesota for introducing me to the art of black and white photography, and the Carleton College Geology Department for the generous use of their maps. I thank my husband and two small boys for accompanying me over steep hills, into damp caves, and along rocky lake shores. My heartiest thanks goes to Zona Meyer, my enthusiastic, patient, and ever-conscientious typist. Each of these persons, and others too numerous to mention, has in his or her own special way supported and aided me in the arduous task of writing this book.

Cover Photo By: George Gambsky and Nancy Campbell

First published by Voyageur Press
9337 Nesbitt Rd., Bloomington, MN 55437

ISBN 0-89658-036-9

First Edition
1 2 3 4 5

To R.C.J. who built the trail,
B.J.J. who pointed it out,
and K.N.S. who traveled it with me.

Rocks of the Duluth Complex, Little Saganaga Lake.

Contents

REGION II—SOUTHEASTERN MINNESOTA
Paleozoic Rocks, Surface Water and Groundwater

REGION III—SOUTHWESTERN MINNESOTA
Till Plain and Ground Moraine, the Minnesota Valley and Archean Rocks

REGION IV—WEST CENTRAL MINNESOTA
Lakes and Moraines

REGION V—NORTHWESTERN MINNESOTA
Glacial Lake Agassiz

REGION VI—EAST CENTRAL MINNESOTA
Confluence of Mississippi, Minnesota, and St. Croix Rivers

Introduction

Why This Book

Minnesota is geologically diverse and unique. Certain rocks in the valley of the Minnesota River are as old as any on earth. The iron-formations of Northeastern Minnesota are classical in type and occurrence. The sedimentary rock of Southeastern Minnesota provides an outstanding record of primitive marine conditions and life. Minnesota's exhibit of glacial features is extraordinary.

This book is the culmination of several years of intense study of Minnesota's outstanding geologic features. During 1980 I inventoried over 500 of the state's noteworthy geologic features for The Nature Conservancy and for the Minnesota Natural Heritage Program. This inventory demanded library research and fieldwork. I spoke with many geologists, soil scientists, naturalists, and outdoor-oriented people. The highlight of this study was an aerial reconnaissance of selected features: during this time I spent three days in a small plane and logged approximately 2200 miles. This experience, combined with my love for the outdoors, knowledge as a geologist, and interests as a teacher, convinced me that a geologic field guide, in particular one for the layperson and family, should be written for Minnesota.

I thus wrote *Minnesota Underfoot*, completing the fieldwork during the fall of 1981 and the spring of 1982. My husband took the photographs. Our two small boys acccompanied us on all the excursions. The book's field research became an extraordinary family experience.

Since *Minnesota Underfoot* is written both for the geologist and the layperson, it should be valuable in the field and also in the classroom. The book provides detailed maps, directions, and descriptions of 56 of Minnesota's most outstanding geologic features. It should be easy to understand and easy to use. It should be of interest to the person on foot or in an automobile, canoe, or armchair. Most importantly, it is designed to be placed in the car—along with fieldglasses, hiking shoes, and camera—ready

1

to facilitate an afternoon's or a month's exploration of the state. Carry it along rocky beaches, up steep bluffs, and into roadside quarries. Let *Minnesota Underfoot* serve as your reference and guide.

Selection of Sites

The selection of sites for this book is based on geologic considerations. Each site is representative of an outstanding geologic feature of Minnesota. Secondary considerations are geographic distribution, reasonable accessibility, and high durability. Most sites are under some sort of public ownership and protection.

Although the fragility of hills and rocks cannot be compared with that of plants and animals, people may nevertheless do a great deal of damage to these unique portions of our natural heritage. Established paths should be used whenever possible, and steep banks should be avoided. Rock hammers should not be used at these sites. Collecting of any sort is discouraged or forbidden. Return from your journeys with photographs and knowledge. Return having seen and understood something of Minnesota's varied landscape.

This book is written in the sincere hope that greater knowledge brings greater respect.

The Book's Organization

I have divided Minnesota into six regions based on geographic location and geologic framework. The geographic location gives the region its title. The geologic framework defines the region. The framework has led to the geographic divisions. Region I, Northeastern Minnesota, is based on the abundant outcrops of Precambrian rock. Region II, Southeastern Minnesota, is based on outcrops of Paleozoic rock and pre-Wisconsin glacial deposits. Region III, Southwestern Minnesota, is defined by a subdued landscape of young, thick glacial drift and occasional outcrops of Precambrian rock. Region IV, West Central Minnesota, is a young glaciated region of almost innumerable hills and lakes and very few rock outcrops. Region V, Northwestern Minnesota, includes the entire Glacial Lake Agassiz plain—the flat agricultural western region and the bog-filled eastern region. Region VI, East Central Minnesota, is a triangular-shaped region at the confluence of the Mississippi, Minnesota, and St. Croix rivers. These rivers cut through young glacial drift, outwash sands, and lake sediments to expose late Precambrian and early Paleozoic rocks.

The regions are numbered in geologic sequence, that is, Northeastern Minnesota taken as a whole is the oldest region of the state. East Central Minnesota is the youngest region. Within each region are a varying number of sites. These sites are numbered in a way that makes the best geologic and geographic sense—generally from oldest to youngest, but also with a consideration for the easiest travel from one site to another. Usually the first site in each region gives an overview of that region.

The text for each site consists of three sections. The first section discusses the geologic importance of the site. The second section gives directions for reaching that site. The third section discusses the site in detail. The site's title consists of two parts: the first describes the feature in geologic terms, the second gives a geographic and cultural identification to the site. Below the title and above the text are listed the county in which the site is located, the nearest town to the site, the ownership of the site, and the United States Geological Survey (USGS) topographic map on which the site may be found.

Sites and text are organized and written in such a manner that they may be visited and read in any order. However, please read the introduction to each region while visiting sites within that region.

Geologic Timetable

Eon	Era	Period	Millions of Years Ago Began	Geologic and Biologic Events
Phanerozoic "Evident Life"	Cenozoic "Age of Mammals"	Quaternary Holocene Pleistocene	1 <.1	Glaciation of northern continents & rise of man
		Tertiary	65	Grasses abundant, rise of mammals
	Mesozoic "Age of Reptiles"	Cretaceous	135	Rocky Mountains begin to form, early flowering plants
		Jurassic	180	Dinosaurs at their zenith
		Triassic	230	Forest of conifers and cycads
	Paleozoic "Ancient Life"	Permian	280	Salt deserts in S.W. U.S.A., early Appalachians
		Carboniferous	345	Extensive coal
		Devonian	405	Fishes abound
		Silurian	425	First land animals
		Ordovician	500	First vertebrates
		Cambrian	600	Earliest abundant sea life
Precambrian—"Before Life"	Proterozoic "Earlier Than Life"	Upper Middle Lower	2600	Scanty record of primitive organisms, iron-formations
	Archean "Ancient"		4000	Rocks much altered and history obscured, no fossils

4   *Introduction*

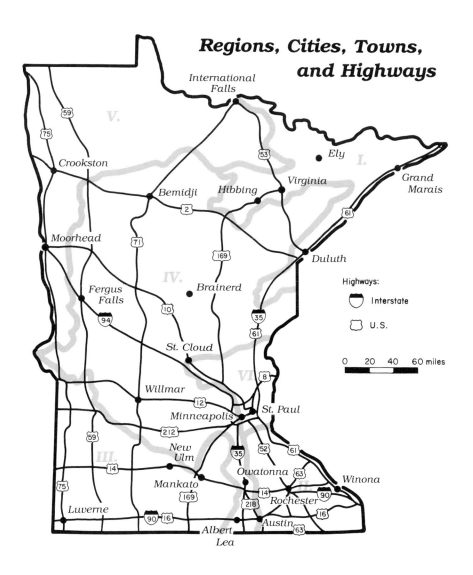

Regions, Cities, Towns, and Highways

International Falls

V.

59
75

Crookston

53

Ely

I.

Virginia

Grand Marais

Bemidji

Hibbing

2

Moorhead

71

169

61

Duluth

Fergus Falls

IV.

Brainerd

Highways:

Interstate

U.S.

10

94

35

61

St. Cloud

0   20   40   60 miles

VI.

8

Willmar

12

New Ulm

Minneapolis

St. Paul

59

212

14

75

Mankato

169

35

52

61

Owatonna

63

Winona

14

90

Luverne

90 16

218

Rochester

16

Albert Lea

Austin

63

Regions and Sites

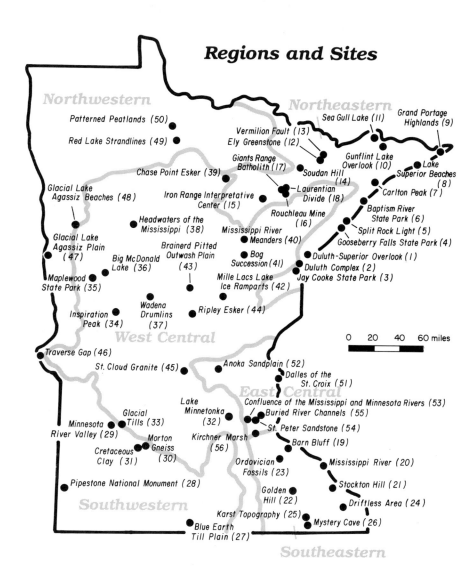

Patterned Peatlands (50)

Red Lake Strandlines (49)

Sea Gull Lake (11)

Grand Portage Highlands (9)

Vermilion Fault (13)
Ely Greenstone (12)

Giants Range Batholith (17)
Chase Point Esker (39)

Soudan Hill (14)

Gunflint Lake Overlook (10)

Lake Superior Beaches (8)

Glacial Lake Agassiz Beaches (48)

Iron Range Interpretative Center (15)

Laurentian Divide (18)

Carlton Peak (7)

Headwaters of the Mississippi (38)

Rouchleau Mine (16)

Baptism River State Park (6)

Mississippi River Meanders (40)

Split Rock Light (5)
Gooseberry Falls State Park (4)

Glacial Lake Agassiz Plain (47)

Brainerd Pitted Outwash Plain (43)

Big McDonald Lake (36)

Bog Succession (41)

Duluth-Superior Overlook (1)
Duluth Complex (2)

Maplewood State Park (35)

Mille Lacs Lake Ice Ramparts (42)

Jay Cooke State Park (3)

Inspiration Peak (34)

Wadena Drumlins (37)

Ripley Esker (44)

Traverse Gap (46)

St. Cloud Granite (45)

Anoka Sandplain (52)

Dalles of the St. Croix (51)

0   20   40   60 miles

Lake Minnetonka (32)

Confluence of the Mississippi and Minnesota Rivers (53)

Buried River Channels (55)

St. Peter Sandstone (54)

Glacial Tills (33)

Minnesota River Valley (29)

Morton Gneiss (30)

Kirchner Marsh (56)

Barn Bluff (19)

Cretaceous Clay (31)

Ordovician Fossils (23)

Mississippi River (20)

Pipestone National Monument (28)

Golden Hill (22)

Stockton Hill (21)

Driftless Area (24)

Karst Topography (25)

Mystery Cave (26)

Blue Earth Till Plain (27)

Notes on the Reading of Topographic Maps, Geologic Timetables, and Stratigraphic Columns

Topographic maps, the geologic timetable, and the Minnesota stratigraphic column are an integral part of this book. Take time to look carefully at these illustrations and to learn a bit about them. Consult them frequently. A topographic map is included for every site in the book. The geologic timetable is found *on page 4;* the Minnesota stratigraphic column, *on page 14.*

Topographic maps are maps on which are placed the important cultural and physical features of the land. Rivers and streams, lakes, highways, and cities are found on these maps. Most importantly, the maps show hills, plains, and valleys. These landforms are indicated by the use of contour lines, thin wavy lines connecting points of equal elevation. Contour lines may be placed at any contour interval. In this book they are placed at intervals of five, 10, 20, 50 and 100 feet. Every fifth contour line is labeled. To get the elevation of a particular contour line, interpolate between the labeled lines. To get the elevation of a particular place not on a contour line, interpolate between the neighboring lines. The easiest way to understand a topographic map is to find a naturally low area, such as a lake or stream, and follow the contour lines away and upward form that point: imagine yourself walking across the map. Note that north is always up on a topographic map and that the scale varies.

The topographic maps all come from the U.S. Geological Survey and may be ordered by writing: Eastern Distribution Branch, U.S. Geological Survey, 1200 S. Eads St., Arlington, Virginia 22202. They may also be bought at the Minnesota Geological Survey at 2610 University Ave., St. Paul, Minnesota 55114.

A geologic timetable is a table which orders geologic time. The oldest segments of geologic time are placed at the bottom of the table—moving upward the segments become progressively younger. A standard and simplified geologic timetable is found *on page 4.* Note that all geologic time is divided into three major eons: from the oldest to the youngest these are the Archean, the Proterozoic, and the Phanerozoic. The Archean and Proterozoic are often known as the Precambrian or "time before life." The Phanerozoic is known as the "time of evident life." Each eon is divided into several eras, and each era into several periods. This geologic timetable also indicates how long ago each period began and the significant geologic and biologic events that occurred during that time.

The Minnesota stratigraphic column, found *on page 14,* is a geologic ordering of Minnesota's rocks: the oldest rocks are at the bottom and the youngest rocks at the top. Note that the geologic time divisions in this table correspond to those in the geologic timetable. However, the stratigraphic, or rock, column is only a partial time column: it is simply the sequence of rocks in a particular region. Refer frequently to this column and compare it to the geologic timetable. A great deal of information is found by comparing the two. For instance, the Jordan Sandstone was laid down in the Cambrian, the time of earliest abundant sea life. The rock is thus between 500 and 600 million years old and is close in age to the St. Lawrence Formation.

A Geologic Overview of Minnesota

Minnesota lies at the center of North America. It has a varied landscape of bare rock and rich agricultural soil, hill and plain, ravine and knife-edge ridge, river and lake, prairie and forest. The state encompasses 84,068 square miles of land and 4779 square miles of water. It sits astride the Superior Upland, a portion of the ancient, long-eroded rock core of North America, and the Central Lowlands, a geologically younger region of gentle hills and plains.

Minnesota's surface waters flow north into the Arctic, east into the Atlantic, and south into the Gulf of Mexico. North America's largest river system, the Mississippi, begins in Minnesota.

Most of Minnesota's land surface is gently rolling. However, the elevation of the land ranges from 602 feet on the shore of Lake Superior to 2301 feet at the top of Eagle Mountain in central Cook County. The greatest local relief is found along Lake Superior. An elevation change of greater than 800 feet often occurs within three miles of the shore. Local relief surpasses 450 feet along the Mississippi River bluffs south of Winona and occasionally over 300 feet in the belts of glacial hills throughout west central Minnesota. The least relief, less than 10 feet, occurs in northwestern Minnesota on the old Agassiz lake plain.

Crustal unrest, wind, water, and ice have all played their roles in building and sculpturing this land. Periods of active mountain building have been followed by times of relative quiet. Shallow seas have given way to rivers, streams, and glaciers. Gentle breezes have been followed by howling winds.

During the Precambrian—the interval of geologic time which ended 600 million years ago—all of these geologic forces acted on Minnesota. Mountains were built and destroyed, seas came and went, rivers grew and disappeared. A record of these events is left in the ancient crystalline and clastic (fragmental) rocks exposed in northeastern and southwestern Minnesota.

During the Paleozoic, a time of relative quiet, shallow continental seas moved back and forth across much of the state. All but northeastern Minnesota and a small portion of southwestern Minnesota are underlain by the soft clastic and carbonate rocks deposited at this time.

The late Paleozoic, much of the Mesozoic, and most of the Cenozoic were times of equitable climate, slow uplift of the land, and gentle erosion of older rocks by wind and water.

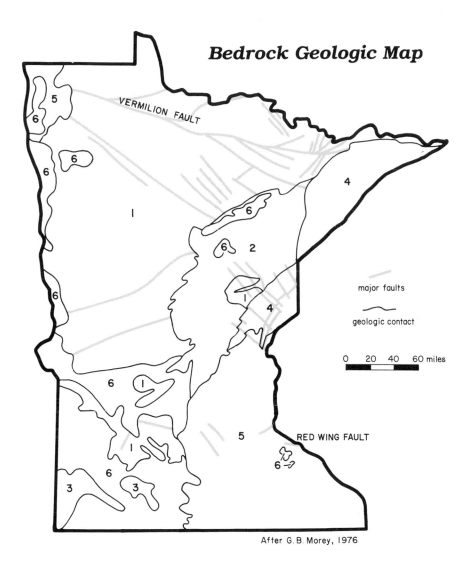

Bedrock Geologic Map

VERMILION FAULT

5

6

6

6

1

6

6

2

6

1

4

4

major faults

geologic contact

0   20   40   60 miles

6

1

5

RED WING FAULT

3

6

3

6

After G.B. Morey, 1976

6	Upper Mesozoic Rocks: Cretaceous sediments
5	Lower Paleozoic Sedimentary Rocks: sandstone, shale, dolomite, limestone; primarily Ordovician & Cambrian rocks (Devonian carbonates in extreme southern Minnesota)
4	Middle Proterozoic Rocks: North Shore Volcanics, Duluth Complex, and other igneous and sedimentary rocks
3	Lower Proterozoic Sioux Quartzite
2	Lower Proterozoic Rocks: granitic rocks, shale, sandstone, quartzite, iron-formation, basalt, dolomite; most rocks are weakly to moderately metamorphosed
1	Archean Rocks: granitic rocks, metasedimentary and metaigneous rocks, greenstone, some iron-formation

The climate changed dramatically during the Pleistocene, or Ice Age. Beginning approximately two million years ago, ice sheets, or glaciers, up to a mile thick repeatedly invaded Minnesota. Glacial deposits now cover most of the state: unsorted clays, silts, sands, and gravels. Huge boulders, some of them glacially transported far from their place of origin, litter many fields.

By approximately 10,000 years ago, Minnesota was once again ice free. Warmer and drier conditions prevailed. Organic matter began to fill depressions left by the glaciers. Streams began again to branch across and drain the land. Tundra vegetation, then forest and prairie grew in succession on the barren ground.

Today we have broken the prairie sod, cut the forest, and harnessed the streams. We have drained marshes, planed hills, and modified the soils. But our achievements become insignificant when contrasted to glacial advance, sea encroachment, mountain building, and the constant erosion of streams. Our total existence is but a wink in geologic time.

Minnesota's Outstanding Geologic Features

Minnesota's most outstanding geologic features may be placed in one or more of the following categories: 1) Precambrian rocks, 2) early Paleozoic sedimentary rocks, 3) Cretaceous clays, 4) glacial landforms, 5) postglacial landforms, 6) lakes and wetlands, 7) rivers and streams, 8) groundwater solution features, and 9) fossils. Some of these features are unique in a national or international sense. Others are simply extraordinary examples of commonplace geologic occurrences—processes, landforms, rocks.

The Precambrian rocks exposed in northeastern and southwestern Minnesota are all older than 600 million years. The oldest of these rocks, those found in the Minnesota River valley and in Kanabec County, are greater than 3.5 billion years. These latter rocks may be the world's oldest, equaled or surpassed only by those of West Greenland. Minnesota's Precambrian rocks are also remarkable for their variable composition. The rocks of Morton, Duluth, and Pigeon Point have been studied extensively in an effort to understand the causes of this variation. The Minnesota iron-formations, once containing one of the world's greatest concentrations of iron ore, are also of Precambrian age.

Early Paleozoic rocks are exposed throughout southeastern Minnesota along the Mississippi River and its tributaries. These rocks were laid down layer upon layer in shallow continental seas. In them is a detailed record of the changing physical, chemical, and biological conditions of 400 million to 600 million years ago.

Cretaceous clays, formed under moist, semitropical conditions, are exposed in the vicinity of Redwood Falls. These clays, as much as 100 feet

Physiography and Drainage Basins

Rainy River

Pigeon River

AGASSIZ LAKE PLAIN

RAINY RIVER BASIN

Upper & Lower Red Lakes

BORDER LAKES

Red River of the North

RED RIVER BASIN

IRON RANGES

NORTH SHORE HIGHLANDS

Lake Superior

ITASCA MORAINE

LAKE SUPERIOR BASIN

BRAINERD PITTED OUTWASH PLAIN

Mille Lacs Lake

ST. CROIX RIVER BASIN

drainage divide

MISSISSIPPI RIVER BASIN

St. Croix

0   20   40   60 miles

BIG STONE MORAINE

ALEXANDRIA MORAINE

ANOKA SANDPLAIN

Mississippi

Minnesota River

ST. CROIX MORAINE

OWATONNA MORAINE

River

Lake Pepin

COTEAU DES PRAIRIES

MINNESOTA RIVER BASIN

Root River

BLUE EARTH TILL PLAIN

DRIFTLESS AREA

Modified from Wright, in Sims and Morey, 1972

MISSOURI RIVER BASIN

DES MOINES RIVER BASIN

thick, consist of material derived through the extreme weathering of the underlying Precambrian rock. Similar clays are forming today on Victoria Island, Hong Kong. Both materials have been studied in an attempt to understand and document the breakdown of surface rocks under particular climatic conditions and over long periods of time.

Glacial landforms are found throughout Minnesota. Glaciers, perhaps the greatest determinant of Minnesota's landscape, have left their mark virtually everywhere. The ice scoured certain regions and on melting deposited material in others. A myriad of landforms resulted: elongate hills, rounded knobs, irregular depressions, undulating plains, and sinuous ridges. As the glaciers melted, large lakes and vast outwash fans, plains of meltwater-deposited sand, developed along their margins. Glacial meltwaters greatly widened preexisting valleys and carved steep-sided rock gorges.

Postglacial landforms caused by wind and ice are also common throughout Minnesota. Wind removed and rearranged the sands and silts on barren plains left by the receding ice. Dunes, as in northern Anoka County, and silt-capped hills, as near Cannon Falls, have resulted. Lake ice exerting pressure on nearby land has pushed lakeshore materials into long, low ridges called ice ramparts. Lakes of the Brainerd and Detroit Lakes regions are especially renowned for these features.

Minnesota's lakes were formed in many ways. Minnesota's wetlands were formed through the postglacial accumulation of undecomposed plant material. The most extraordinary of these lakes are Glacial Lake Agassiz, Lake Superior, and the border lakes. Glacial Lake Agassiz, a huge ice-margin lake, once covered portions of Minnesota, North Dakota, Saskatchewan, Manitoba, and Ontario. Its abandoned beaches document the waning stages of Minnesota's latest glaciation. Lake Superior, the world's largest freshwater lake, records within its sediments and along its shores glacial and postglacial events—the waxing and waning of several ice sheets and the subsequent uplift of the land. The border lakes testify to the degree to which wind, water, and ice can erode solid rock—their varying shapes and depths resulting from differing rock composition and inclination. Minnesota's almost innumerable other lakes are primarily the result of unequal deposition or collapse of glacial drift, unsorted rock material, and outwash. Buried in their bottom sediment is a record of postglacial climate. Minnesota's wetlands have developed where vegetative growth and organic accumulation have filled in smaller, shallower lake basins. The accumulating organic matter has resulted in vast peat deposits northeast of Aitkin and north of Upper Red Lake. The vegetative growth and accumulating organic matter have also resulted in Minnesota's numerous sphagnum bogs, tamarack swamps, and cattail marshes.

Minnesota's rivers and streams, especially the Mississippi, Minnesota, and St. Croix, exhibit a great variety of features. These features again record glacial, postglacial, and recent geologic events. The Mississippi, at present draining over three quarters of the state, has over its long history cut numerous channels through glacial material and bedrock. An entire network of buried river channels underlies the Twin Cities. The Minnesota River, actually an integral part of the Mississippi, has a fascinating history. This river, once much larger than today and called Glacial River Warren, served as the outlet stream for Glacial Lake Agassiz. For several thousand years this enormous roaring stream coursed across central Minnesota, cutting a huge rock channel all the way from Browns Valley to St. Paul. Rock terraces mark the varying stages of the river's erosion, and scoured rock islands indicate indicate the magnitude and erosive power of that river. Today the Minnesota's immense valley, dwarfing the present stream, stands in mute but eloquent testimony to this magnificent and turbulent past. The St. Croix River, once the pathway for waters of the Lake Superior basin, is bordered near Taylors Falls by a large rock gorge and dozens of giant potholes.

Groundwater solution features are common in extreme southeastern Minnesota. Groundwater there has played an important role in landscape development. Glacial drift is virtually nonexistent, and Paleozoic limestone appears at or near the surface. The limestone is highly soluble, even in the weak carbonic acid formed from rain and carbon dioxide. Over millions of years it has become riddled with caverns, sinks (holes), and caves. Near Harmony, Spring Valley, and Preston, sinks may be seen dotting the corn and alfalfa fields. In the same vicinity are several commercially operated caves.

Fossils are found throughout Minnesota. They are an extraordinary record of physical, biological, and climatic conditions far different from those of today. Fossils of earliest life are found in the Precambrian rocks in northeastern Minnesota. These simple one-celled organisms lived in ocean shallows, manufacturing their food from sunlight and seawater. A diverse and well-preserved assemblage of primitive marine animals is found in the early Paleozoic rocks. These animals, both single and multicelled, lived in shallow, well-lit, semitropical seas. More recent plant fossils buried in postglacial lake sediments document the spread and retreat of Minnesota's forests and grasslands. Conifer and hardwood forests, as well as short- and long-grass prairie, have each grown in response to changing postglacial climate. Fossils of all kinds have been used to reconstruct and date various geologic events.

Minnesota Stratigraphic Column

Era	Period	Epoch	Stage	Stratigraphic Unit
				[Note: The Cretaceous, Proterozoic, and Archean listings imply nothing of the rock's stratigraphic sequence or relationship. All Paleozoic formations are in stratigraphic sequence.]
PHANEROZOIC (EON)				
Cenozoic	Quaternary	Holocene		alluvium, peat
		Holocene and Pleistocene		redistributed material (glacial lake deposits, terraces, loess)
		Pleistocene	Late Wisconsin	Des Moines Lobe drift Superior Lobe drift—Rainy Lobe drift—Wadena Lobe drift (Itasca area) Wadena Lobe drift (Alexandria area)
			Pre–Late Wisconsin	Granite Falls Drift Old Red Drift (Hampton) Hawk Creek Drift Old Gray Drift residuum
Mesozoic	Cretaceous			Coleraine Formation, Colorado Group, Dakota Group, Windrow Formation
	Jurassic (?)			"Hallock red beds"
Paleozoic	Devonian			Cedar Valley Formation
	Ordovician			Maquoketa Formation Dubuque Formation Galena Formation Decorah Formation Platteville Formation Glenwood Formation St. Peter Sandstone Shakopee Formation Oneota Dolomite
	Cambrian			Jordan Sandstone St. Lawrence Formation Franconia Formation Ironton Sandstone Galesville Sandstone Eau Claire Formation Mt. Simon Sandstone

Minnesota Stratigraphic Column

Time				Stratigraphic Unit
Era	Period	Epoch	Stage	

PROTEROZOIC (EON)

Upper (?)	Fond du Lac Formation, Hinckley Sandstone
Middle	Chengwatana Volcanic Group, Duluth Complex, Fond du Lac Formation (?), Hinckley Sandstone (?), North Shore Volcanics, Puckwunge Formation, Solor Church Formation
Lower	Biwabik Iron Formation, Cedar Mountain Complex, Denham Formation, Glen Township Formation, Gunflint Iron Formation, Hillman Migmatite, Little Falls Formation, Mahnomen Formation, Pokegama Quartzite, Rabbit Lake Formation, Rove Formation, Section 28 Granite, Sioux Quartzite, Stearns Igneous Complex, Thomson Formation, Trommald Formation
ARCHEAN (EON)	Algoman Granite, Couchiching Group, Ely Greenstone, Giants Range Granite, Jasper Lake Volcanic Complex, Keewatin Greenstone, Knife Lake Group, Lake Vermilion Formation, McGrath Gneiss, Montevideo Gneiss, Morton Gneiss, Newton Lake Formation, Sacred Heart Granite, Saganaga Tonalite, Seine Group, Vermilion Granitic Complex

Lake Superior and Precambrian basalt, Gooseberry Falls State Park.

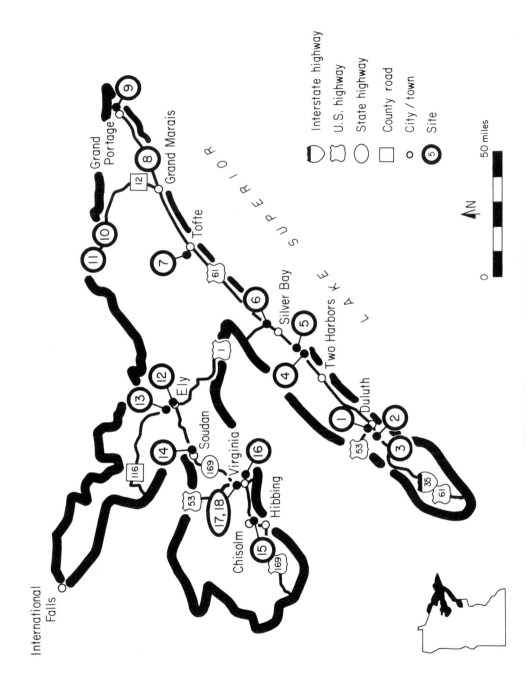

Grand Portage

Grand Marais

International Falls

LAKE SUPERIOR

Tofte

Silver Bay

Two Harbors

Duluth

Ely

Soudan

Virginia

Hibbing

Chisolm

Interstate highway
U.S. highway
State highway
County road
City / town
Site

N

0   50 miles

I Northeastern Minnesota

Precambrian Rocks, Lake Superior, and the Border Lakes

Northeastern Minnesota is a rugged, sparsely populated region of lakes and mountains, brushland and forest. It is dominated by the cold clear waters and high rocky shores of Lake Superior, the small gemlike border lakes, and the red and gray ore-rich rocks of the Mesabi and Vermilion iron ranges. It is defined through the preponderance of exposed Precambrian rock, rocks formed more than 600 million years ago, during earliest geologic time.

This region is bounded on the west by thick deposits of young glacial and lake materials which obscure the underlying Precambrian rocks. This western boundary runs irregularly from Rainy Lake southeastward to Lake Vermilion, westward around the Mesabi Iron Range, back eastward almost to Lake Superior, and then southwestward paralleling the lake to just beyond Duluth. Near Carlton this western boundary swings eastward again and meets Lake Superior at the mouth of the St. Louis River. Northeastern Minnesota is bounded on the north by the international boundary from Rainy Lake to Pigeon Point and on the southeast by Lake Superior.

The rocks of Northeastern Minnesota are a part of the Canadian Shield, a dome-shaped mass of exposed Precambrian rock, the ancient crystalline core of North America. Equivalent rocks and shields are found near the center of each continent. These shield rocks, from both the Archean and Proterozoic eons, cover a time span of almost three billion years and account for seven eighths of all earth's history. During this time the earth developed a solid crust, oceans evolved, and life began. Great sedimentary iron deposits were laid down in shallow seas. Glaciers waxed and waned over the continents. Mountains were built and destroyed.

The sequence of Precambrian rocks in Northeastern Minnesota is one of the most complete and well known in the world. The rocks are well exposed through glacial scour. They are well known through intense geologic exploration, exploration which has been made possible and profitable by the exploitation of rich iron deposits and the continued prospecting for metal ores.

The very oldest rocks of Northeastern Minnesota, Archean in age and as much as 2.7 billion years old, are the granites and greenstones of the border lakes and iron ranges. The youngest rocks are the basalt lavas, dark gabbros, and sandstones of the North Shore. They are Middle and Upper Proterozoic in age and at the least slightly less than one billion years old. The granites, formed from molten material deep within the earth's crust, are seen bordering Lakes Burntside, Saganaga, and Sea Gull. The greenstones, believed to be much altered submarine lava flows, crop out in Ely. The basalts are seen from Duluth to Grand Portage. They are the dark gray and black rocks over which flow the Gooseberry, Baptism, and Cascade rivers. They form many of the points, islands, and promontories of the North Shore. The gabbro, intruded under and into the basalt, crops out in Duluth and along the Gunflint Trail. The sandstones, shallow water deposits, crop out near Fond du Lac southwest of Duluth and along Grand Portage Bay.

Midway in age between the greenstones and the basalts are Minnesota's Proterozoic iron-formations. They crop out from Grand Rapids northeast to Biwabik. Other Lower Proterozoic rocks are seen along the Gunflint Trail near Gunflint Lake and along the St. Louis River in Jay Cooke State Park.

There is little rock material in Northeastern Minnesota younger than the Precambrian. However, in the western part of the Mesabi Iron Range is a thin layer of Cretaceous conglomerate, shale, and sandstone. Glacial tills and outwash also occur sporadically throughout the region, as do heavy red glacial lake clays.

There are no sea-deposited limestones or dolomites. There are few gentle hills and no deep fertile soils. There are no records of early marine animals, the vast Paleozoic coal swamps, or the immense dinosaurs. The rock record of Northeastern Minnesota has a virtual hiatus of almost a billion years. Only the slow weathering and erosion of the ancient Precambrian rocks occurred during most of this interval. It often seems as if much of geologic time has passed by this region and that the glaciers were but an afterthought.

1 Duluth-Superior Overlook

Enger Tower

COUNTY: **St. Louis**
NEAREST TOWN: **Duluth**
OWNERSHIP: **City of Duluth**
USGS TOPOGRAPHIC MAPS: **Duluth, 7½',
1953: Duluth Heights, 7½', 1953**

Enger Tower provides an outstanding panoramic view of the Duluth-Superior area. These cities are situated at the southwest end of Lake Superior at the mouth of the St. Louis River. Duluth sprawls along a prominent ridge of dark Precambrian rock. Superior sits on a low-lying plain of Quaternary lake sediment. Between the two lies the Duluth-Superior Harbor, with its aerial bridge, ships of many nations, and long, bounding sandspit. The drama of this setting—the cities and the ships, harbor and lake, river and rock—is undeniable, its geologic story worth examining.

Enger tower is located in the east end of Duluth's Enger Park. Exit westward on Mesaba Avenue from U.S. Highway 61. Wind to the top of the hill, then turn southwest, left, onto the Skyline Parkway. The Skyline Parkway is one block before the intersection of Mesaba Avenue and Minnesota Highway 194. Follow the parkway southwestward for approximately two miles, then turn right onto a paved but unmarked road. This road lies immediately east of the Enger Park Golf Course. Proceed 0.3 mile, then turn right again at the Enger Tower sign. Proceed another 0.3 mile to the parking area. Adjacent to the parking area is a picnic ground and rock outbuilding. Enger Tower, dark and windowed, is located on the top of the treed slope to the west. Approach the tower by a paved trail and rock steps. Other trails lead eastward to a natural overlook.

Enger Observation Tower, built in the 1930s, is constructed of local rock—red felsite, gray granite, black diabase, basalt, and gabbro. It is dedicated to the memory of Bert J. Enger, "a native of Norway, and citizen of Duluth."

The 62-foot tower stands on a dark knob of gabbro 583 feet above Lake Superior. The view from its top is magnificent.

Northeast of Enger Tower are Lake Superior and the North Shore. Lake Superior, the world's largest freshwater lake, lies in an ice-scoured trough of Precambrian rock. The upturned edge of this basin underlies the conspicuous highland along Minnesota's North Shore. Duluth is built on the southern terminus of this ridge.

Southeast of Enger Tower lies the city of Superior. Its level ground and low-lying position attest to the fact that it is built on an old lake bottom. Lake Superior, once far higher than at present and named Glacial Lake Duluth, flooded the contiguous lowlands. On its floor were deposited heavy red clay and other lake sediments. Along its shores were formed beach terraces and wave-cut cliffs. Lake bottom sediments underlie the city of Superior and much of the area to the southwest. Shorelines hundreds of feet above the present lake are seen in the immediate vicinity of Enger Tower and elsewhere. The Skyline Parkway follows the highest beach, approximately 560 feet above the present lake. Gravel ridges, gravel pits, and wave-cut bluffs mark its presence.

To the east and southeast of Enger Tower lies the Duluth-Superior Harbor. This outstanding natural harbor is a drowned mouth, or estuary, of the St. Louis River. After glacial retreat, the land rose slowly, more to the north where the ice load had been greatest than to the south. The Lake Superior basin thus tilted southward, and its waters flooded the lower portions of the St. Louis and other south shore rivers. The tilting and flooding continue today.

Separating the St. Louis estuary from

Duluth-Superior and vicinity from the USGS Duluth 1:250,000, 1953 (limited revision 1963) map.

Lake Superior are two long, narrow sandspits: Minnesota and Wisconsin points. These points have been built of sand brought into the lake by the St. Louis River and dispersed through a combination of wave action and shore current. The shore current has been set up by the prevailing northeast wind. In back of these points are an older and shorter pair of points, built at an earlier time and in the same way.

Today the level of Lake Superior has been stabilized. However, the southward tilting of the Superior basin cannot be stopped, nor the slow drowning of the St. Louis River, nor the movement of sand along Minnesota Point. Geologic change is slow but inexorable. The view from Enger Tower will change—but don't wait for it.

View northeast from Enger Tower—City of Duluth, Lake Superior, and the North Shore.

Enger Tower, Duluth.

2 Duluth Complex

Magney Park, West Duluth

COUNTY: **St. Louis**
NEAREST TOWN: **Duluth**
OWNERSHIP: **City of Duluth**
USGS TOPOGRAPHIC MAP: **West Duluth, 7½', 1954**

The Duluth Complex is a famous mass of igneous rock which underlies much of the elevated region immediately behind Minnesota's North Shore (the North Shore highland). The peculiar shape and mineral composition of this rock has been studied in great detail. Is the Duluth Complex lens, funnel, or wedge shaped? Does it represent one large intrusion or numerous smaller ones? Has faulting been involved in the rock's origin and evolution? Did its unusual mineral suite become segregated through gravity and flow separation alone or through repeated periods of intrusion, cooling, and faulting? One of the most extensive and scenic exposures of the Duluth Complex is near Bardon Peak at Magney Park, where there are miles of open rock hiking.

Magney Park is situated on the south end of the prominent rock ridge which runs along the North Shore and through Duluth. It overlooks the St. Louis River valley. From Interstate 35, 0.5 mile west of the Duluth city limits, follow exit 249 onto the Skyline Parkway. Turn left immediately and follow the parkway southward for 4.1 miles, past Spirit Mountain and onto gravel. Park near the sharp, unmarked turn to the north. Follow a small trail southward onto the rocks.

The rocks of Bardon Peak consist of weathered, dark, gray-green gabbro, the common olivine and feldspar-rich rock of the Duluth Complex. The rock here has been exposed, smoothed, and rounded through long periods of erosion and glacial scour. Since glacial retreat, flat gray-green and yellow-orange lichens have grown on and partially covered the rock's surface.

The Duluth Complex formed during middle Proterozoic time, approximately 1.1 billion years ago (Phinney, *in* Sims and Morey, 1972, p. 333). At that time molten material forced its way into and under the earlier basalt flows of the North Shore Volcanic Group (Site #6). This process, called intrusion, was the culmination of a long period of igneous activity in the western Lake Superior region (Taylor, 1963, p. 4).

Three quarters to nine tenths of the Duluth Complex consists of the unusual rocks gabbro and troctolite, dark-colored, coarse-grained rocks lacking in the common mineral quartz and consisting of large amounts of the minerals plagioclase, olivine, augite, and magnetite-ilmenite. At Duluth, there are, however, gradations from very dark rocks at the base of the complex to very light rocks at its top. Within the gabbro itself are layers of differing mineral composition and texture.

The rocks of the Duluth Complex crop out throughout Duluth, west toward Fond du Lac, and sporadically northeast for 120 miles into central Cook County. There are numerous good exposures of this rock along Duluth's Skyline Parkway. There are other exposures along the northern portion of the Gunflint Trail near the Cross River. Similar rocks crop out in northern Wisconsin and Michigan.

For many years the Duluth Complex was believed to be saucer shaped and was known as a lopolith. It was frequently compared with and contrasted to the world's other famous lopoliths—the Bushveld Complex of South Africa, the Sudbury Complex of Ontario, and the Stillwater Complex of Montana. Today the Duluth Complex is believed to be wedge shaped, confined to a complicated set of related fractures along a large rift, a continent-sized fault system (see Site #51) (Weiblen and Morey, 1980, p. 117). The Duluth Complex, once believed to be a single large intrusive body, is believed to consist of multiple intrusions along this fracture system. Its unusual and complex mineral suite is believed now to have arisen through the separation of heavier and larger crystals by weight and motion and through multiple periods of intrusion, cooling, faulting, and perhaps differing parent magmas.

Most of the current theories on the Duluth Complex have arisen in the past five years, and the complex is still under geologic scrutiny. Many questions are still unanswered concerning the origin, structure, and composition of this unusual rock unit. Perhaps the most pressing of these questions concerns the rock's mineral composition and its economic potential. Within the Duluth Complex have been found traces of copper, iron, nickel, and titanium.

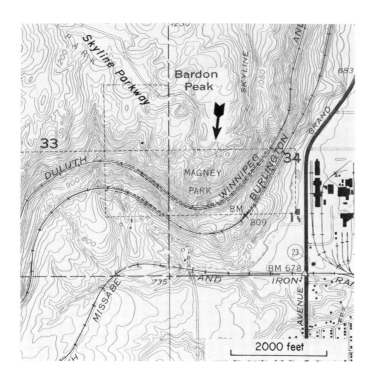

Duluth Gabbro outcrop on Bardon Peak, Magney Park, West Duluth. This view looks south over the St. Louis River valley.

Structural Features in Precambrian Rock

Jay Cooke State Park

COUNTY: **Carlton**
NEAREST TOWN: **Thomson**
OWNERSHIP: **State of Minnesota**
USGS TOPOGRAPHIC MAPS: **Cloquet, 7½',
1954; Esko, 7½", 1954**

Common structural features of Precambrian rock are seen in the ominously dark rocks of Jay Cooke State Park. Here the St. Louis River has cut through young glacial sediments and exposed jagged and tilted beds of ancient slate. Through their variation in composition and structure, these ancient rocks tell much about their original and subsequent environments. In addition to rocks, Jay Cooke State Park offers excellent and varied hiking trails, picnic grounds, and campgrounds.

Jay Cooke State Park is located between the villages of Thomson and Fond du Lac. Take the Carlton-Cromwell exit from Interstate 35 approximately 10 miles south of Duluth. Proceed eastward on Minnesota Highway 210 for 5.2 miles to the town of Carlton. Continue through Carlton and toward Thomson, crossing over the St. Louis River immediately below the Thomson reservoir and dam. At the town of Thomson, continue following Highway 210 as it makes a sharp right turn and 0.5 mile later enters Jay Cooke State Park. Follow this winding road for approximately three miles along the north side of the St. Louis River. Park near the picnic area and information building, examine the information signs, and walk down to the river and across the swinging bridge.

Below and nearby the swinging bridge are tilted slates belonging to the Precambrian Thomson Formation.

These rocks were formed from marine muds approximately two billion years ago (Taylor, 1964, p. 2). After deposition and deep burial, the muds were compressed to become shales and later further compressed and hardened by heat and pressure to become dark, thin-bedded slates. Still further pressure folded the slates and turned them on end. A small fold is visible below the Thomson dam beneath the Minnesota Highway 210 bridge. Tilting is visible throughout the park.

After folding and tilting, molten rock material forced its way into cracks in the Thomson Slate, then cooled and hardened into igneous dikes. A large, white quartz dike is seen near the fold below the highway bridge, and dark diabase dikes are seen scattered throughout the area of the swinging bridge. The latter dikes are much the same color as the enclosing slate but somewhat harder and more resistant to erosion. One diabase dike runs southwestward across the river channel, beginning at the north end of the swinging bridge and ending just east of the nearby bedrock island. This dike is approximately 65 feet wide (Schwartz and Thiel, 1954, p. 238).

Other structures seen within these rocks include rain prints, mud cracks, and ripple marks. The ripple marks are by far the most common. They are seen immediately west of the swinging bridge near its north end, and look like small elongate dimples on the rocks' surface. The ripple marks were formed in the soft muds on the bottom of a Precambrian sea.

Through their structure and composition, these ancient rocks demonstrate that two billion years ago things were not so different from what they are today. Rain fell, shallow seas deposited mud, waves rippled the mud's surface. Mud cracked on drying, and once buried became shale and then slate. However, these rocks show no sign of life: two billion years ago the marine environment was geologically

3

much the same as it is today—biologically it was practically sterile.

Precambrian rocks are the focal point of Jay Cooke State Park. However, there is more to the geologic story here. The high, smooth rock ridges seen near the campground are *roches moutonnées*, or "sheep back" rocks. They were produced through glacial scour less than 50,000 years ago. The uniform red clay, about 10,000 years old, seen near Oldenburg Point, several miles downstream from the swinging bridge, is the basinal deposit of Glacial Lake Duluth (see Site #1), an early ancestor of Lake Superior. Therefore, rocks several billion years old and sediments only several thousand years old both exist at Jay Cooke State Park. The rocks tell the story of ancient seas and deep burial. The sediments tell the story of a glacial lake.

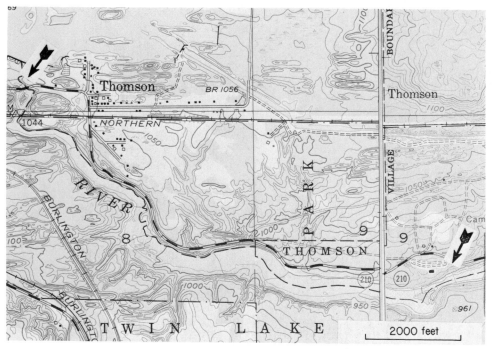

A portion of Jay Cooke State Park and the nearby Thomson reservoir.

St. Louis River cutting through tilted beds of the Precambrian Thomson Formation near the swinging bridge at Jay Cooke State Park.

4 Basalt Lava Flows

Gooseberry Falls State Park

COUNTY: **Lake**
NEAREST TOWN: **Castle Danger**
OWNERSHIP: **State of Minnesota**
USGS TOPOGRAPHIC MAP: **Split Rock Point, 7½', 1956**

Gooseberry Park's low, gently sloping, dark rock points and cascading waterfalls characterize much of Minnesota's North Shore. The rocks, which appear to slide under the waters of Lake Superior and over which plunge the Gooseberry and other North Shore rivers, are hardened basalt lava flows similar to those occurring today on the island of Iceland. These North Shore flows, however, are over one billion years old. Gooseberry Park's picnic ground is located on the surface of one of these ancient flows. River paths and overlooks provide views of other flow surfaces and cross sections. Also included within this 1300-acre park, one of Minnesota's most popular parks, is a large campground and an exceptional information center. There is enough space and enough objects of interest within this park for the young and old alike.

Gooseberry Falls State Park is located 12 miles east of Two Harbors along U.S. Highway 61. It includes the entire scenic rocky gorge and mouth of the Gooseberry River. Two major waterfalls are included in the park, and numerous smaller cascades. Park along the highway near the bridge and follow the steps and trails down along the river. Drive into the picnic ground and hike along the Lake Superior shore.

Almost all the rocks exposed within Gooseberry State Park are basalt lava flows. Basalt is a dark, fine-grained, extrusive igneous rock. There are at least 30 flows within the park, and they range in thickness from one foot to more than 60 feet (Schwartz, 1948, p. 19). These flows are a part of the North Shore Volcanics (Site #6) and fill a large dish-shaped structure, approximately 150 miles wide, under the west end of Lake Superior. The "dish" tilts gently southeastward toward the lake. The park's entire shoreline is edged by this gently sloping rock.

During the late Precambrian, these lavas flowed from large fissures within the earth. For hundreds of thousands of years the dark viscous basalt spread out slowly over Minnesota's North Shore, Michigan's Upper Peninsula, and down into East Central Minnesota along what is now the St. Croix Valley. Layer on layer of this dark lava poured out on the earth and eventually attained a total thickness of around 23,000 feet (Sims and Morey, *in* Sims and Morey, 1972, p. 11).

The upper parts of these lava flows are vesicular, that is, they are filled with holes, cavities from gas bubbles trapped within the lava. Before cooling, the gas bubbles moved upward, collecting near the chilled upper surfaces of the flows. Later the vesicles filled with various minerals, including agate. The filled vesicles are known as amygdules. Note the vesicles and the amygdules in the rock at the base of the stone stairs southwest of the bridge. Also note them at the top of the lower falls and along the Lake Superior shore.

The vesicular tops of the flows are softer and more easily eroded than the massive central portion. Thus a cliff or waterfall develops when the central portion is undercut by erosion on the upper surface of the underlying flow. Such cliffs and waterfalls are seen along Lake Superior and the river. This situation has occurred all up and down the North Shore, each time producing cliffs, points, coves, waterfalls, and cascades—cliffs near the Baptism River, points and coves near the Brule River, waterfalls and cascades along the Temperance River. Ancient basalt lava flows account for much of the North Shore's varied scenery.

Precambrian basalt flows dipping into Lake Superior at the picnic area, Gooseberry Falls State Park.

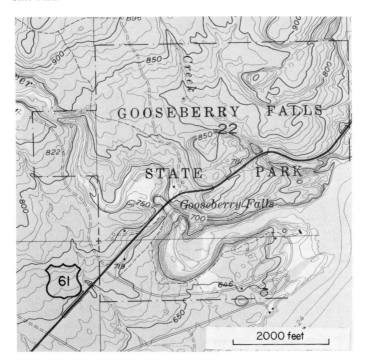

5 North Shore of Lake Superior

Split Rock Light, Vantage Point

COUNTY: **Lake**
NEAREST TOWN: **Beaver Bay**
OWNERSHIP: **State of Minnesota**
USGS TOPOGRAPHIC MAP: **Split Rock Point NE, 7½', 1956; Split Rock Point, 7½', 1956**

There are several high, prominent rocky points along the Lake Superior shore between the Gooseberry and the Baptism rivers. Perhaps the best known of these points is the bold diabase cliff on which is perched Split Rock Lighthouse, a functioning beacon for mariners from 1910 to 1963. From the point and the lighthouse may be obtained an excellent view of both Lake Superior, the world's largest body of freshwater, and the North Shore, a scenic, rocky tourist mecca.

Split Rock Light in Split Rock Lighthouse State Park is located approximately six miles south of Beaver Bay. The entrance road is on the southeast side of U.S. Highway 61. Follow this road to the parking lot, then follow the marked trail southward to the lighthouse. Climb into the lighthouse for a magnificent view of Lake Superior and the North Shore. Lake Superior, immense, clear, and cold, stretches to the horizon on the east, northeast, and southeast. Only on a very clear day can the low-lying sandstone islands of the Apostle group be seen clustering around Wisconsin's Bayfield Peninsula far to the southeast. The next landfall to the east is Sault Ste. Marie, over 300 miles away. Far to the northeast is Isle Royale and Canada. To the southwest is Little Two Harbors, Day Hill, Corundum Point, and Split Rock Point.

Descend from the lighthouse and walk eastward toward the cyclone fence, then look northward along the Superior shore toward other diabase cliffs and points. Return westward, pass the lighthouse, and descend to the shore along a lovely trail through paper birch and bracken fern. From the shore there is an excellent perspective on the lighthouse and point. The dark, resistant, medium-grained diabase, which makes up the bulk of the point, may also be examined here.

Lake Superior is the world's largest freshwater lake, 383 miles long and 160 miles wide. It is also very deep, attaining a depth of 1302 feet. Lake Superior is located in a downward fold, or trough, of Precambrian rock; however, its geologic development has not been simple. The Lake Superior basin has resulted from a combination of geologic events. Faults alongside the trough changed and exaggerated its dimensions. The trough may have partially filled with soft sediments which were later removed through river and then glacial erosion. During glacial retreat meltwaters filled this basin far above present levels. Then as outlets to the south and east opened, the lake level subsided. Eventually the lake reached its present configuration and surface elevation of 602 feet above sea level.

Lake Superior is today an immense, rock-bound lake, capable of piling ice high against the shore and producing ocean-sized currents and waves. Ice, currents, and the ceaseless splash and grind of normal wave action have continuously modified the lake's rocky shores.

The erosion of relatively soft lakeward-dipping basalt flows form the gentle sloping shores seen so clearly at Gooseberry Falls State Park (Site #4) and much of the way between Duluth and Two Harbors. Harder, thicker, more resistant diabase, anorthosite, and rhyolite result in the far more rugged and bolder shoreline seen here at Split Rock Lighthouse State Park and in the vicinity of Baptism River State Park (Site #6).

The high points and headlands near Split Rock Light are composed of both the massive, resistant diabase and anorthosite. Farther north, near the Baptism River, the Big and Little Palisades are composed of thick rhyolite flows. Near the Manitou River, basalt flows again produce a gently sloping shore. In the vicinity of Grand Portage (Site #9) resistant diabase has led to an abrupt, mountainous shore.

This varying combination of rock and water, immobility and fluidity—the opposition of two primal elements—has evoked an endless fascination with the North Shore of Lake Superior.

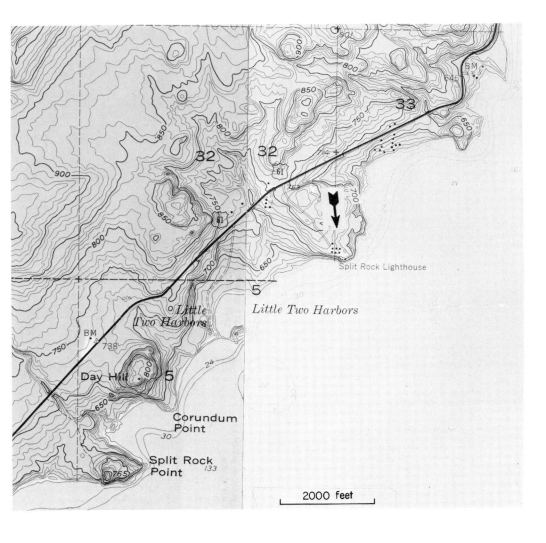

Lake Superior, bold diabase point, and Split Rock Lighthouse.

View of Lake Superior and the North Shore, looking northeast near Split Rock Lighthouse.

6 North Shore Volcanics

Baptism River State Park

COUNTY: **Lake**
NEAREST TOWN: **Illgen City**
OWNERSHIP: **State of Minnesota**
USGS TOPOGRAPHIC MAP: **Illgen City, 7½′, 1956**

The North Shore Volcanics are extrusive and intrusive rocks formed during the middle Proterozoic, over a billion years ago. They consist of basalt flows, rhyolite flows and sills, diabase dikes, and various volcanic tuffs and breccias. This great variety of rocks has led to Baptism River State Park's diverse landscape of waterfalls, rapids, sea arches, sea caves, points, and coves. The most prominent rock, however, is the thick red rhyolite which makes up Shovel Point. Hiking trails run throughout the park, along the rocky gorge of the Baptism River to the gravel bars at the river's mouth and out to the far end of Shovel Point.

Baptism River State Park is located approximately one mile south of Illgen City and eight miles northeast of Beaver Bay. U.S. Highway 61 cuts through this park, which includes the lower portion and mouth of the Baptism River and the adjacent rugged Lake Superior coast. Park on the south side of the highway east of the river and walk northward along the river, then southward to the river's mouth. Make a particular effort to hike at least partway out Shovel Point, following a well-used, relatively easy, and very scenic trail eastward from the parking lot and along the shore. Be prepared to spend several hours exploring this area.

Within Baptism River State Park, the Baptism River has cut a rocky gorge into the North Shore Volcanics. Upstream from the highway bridge the river has cut through numerous gray basalt flows

and reddish rhyolite flows, plunging over these flows in a series of waterfalls and cascades. There are over 20 lava flows in the first two miles upstream from the highway. Downstream, between the highway and the Lake Superior shore, are more basalt flows, several large diabase dikes, and various broken volcanic rocks known as breccia. At the mouth of the Baptism River there are low cliffs composed of rhyolite.

The high and rugged coast of Lake Superior in the vicinity of Baptism River State Park is due to the diversity and resistance of various rocks within the North Shore Volcanics: large, resistant diabase intrusions and rhyolite sills are interspersed with softer rhyolite and basalt flows. The volcanic rocks, cropping out along the shore and eroding differentially produce cliffs and caves, headlands and coves. Immediately southwest of the park is high, prominent Palisade Head—a large rhyolite sill. Within most of the park is a sharp, irregular shore of diabase, rhyolite, and basalt. Along the east side of the park is another large rhyolite sill, elongate Shovel Point.

The Big and Little Palisades—Palisade Head and Shovel Point—bear closer examination. They are both porphyritic rhyolite sills and prominent headlands edged by high, vertical cliffs. Rhyolite is a fine-grained, reddish-colored igneous rock. Since there are larger, light-colored crystals of quartz and feldspar also within the rock it is called porphyritic rhyolite. A sill is any igneous rock which is intruded into and between layers of older rock. These rhyolite sills intruded into older basalt flows. Both sills are edged by high vertical cliffs and undercut by sea arches and caves. The rock has broken and fallen into the lake as waves have cut into the softer, underlying basalt.

The rocks of Baptism River State Park, although belonging to the same rock formation as those of Gooseberry Falls State Park (Site #4), are far more diverse. Only by walking along and among these rocks can their lithologic variation and resulting landscape significance be fully appreciated.

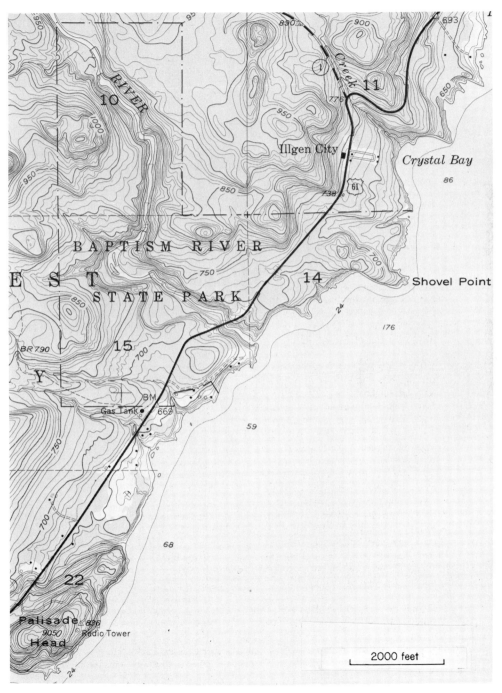

Shovel Point, a large rhyolite sill, at Baptism River State Park.

Anorthosite

Carlton Peak, Cook County

COUNTY: **Cook**
NEAREST TOWN: **Tofte**
OWNERSHIP: **Private; view from forest service road**
USGS TOPOGRAPHIC MAPS: **Schroeder, 7½',
1955; Tofte, 7½', 1955**

Carlton Peak, a landmark in the vicinity of Tofte, is a large rounded anorthosite knob. Anorthosite is an unusual and uncommon rock composed almost entirely of the mineral labradorite, a plagioclase feldspar. The rock is coarse grained and, where fresh, a uniform transparent light green. The peak, one of several in this vicinity composed of anorthosite, rises to 924 feet above Lake Superior and consists of two large and several smaller masses of the anorthosite. There is an excellent view of this peak from forest service road 343. This view is particularly outstanding at the height of fall color, usually the second or third week in September. The rock may be examined up close in Grand Marais.

Forest service road 343 branches northward from U.S. Highway 61 approximately three miles southwest of Tofte, 1.1 miles northeast of Schroeder. This road runs along the Temperance River, adjacent to the Temperance River State Park. Follow the road northward for approximately 1.5 miles, then look to the northeast where Carlton Peak rises sharply above the surrounding trees. From this position is seen the steep, bare, western face of the peak. The gentler northern face is seen from the Sawbill Trail, several miles north of Tofte.

The top of the peak is gently rounded, with bare rock and scattered trees. Partway up the peak and cut into its southern side is a large anorthosite quarry. Much of the rock from this quarry was used for the breakwater at Taconite Harbor. The public was once invited to climb to the top of this peak and may well be again soon; the forest service is hoping to obtain an access trail.

Anorthosite masses occur sporadically all the way from Duluth to Grand Portage; however, most occur between Split Rock and Tofte. The larger masses, highly resistant to erosion, form prominent rounded hills. These anorthosite knobs and masses are a part of the Duluth Complex (Site #2).

Although common in Northeastern Minnesota, anorthosite is rare elsewhere in the world. There are, however, other notable occurrences in New York, Quebec, Labrador, and Norway. Anorthosite has been the subject of intense study because of its rarity and limited mineral composition.

Anorthosite contains 80%–99% labradorite, $Na,Ca(AlSi_3O_8)_2$. At Carlton Peak the anorthosite is 94% labradorite, with crystals commonly one to two inches long. There are a few smaller-crystalled accessory minerals: augite $(Ca(Mg,Fe,Al)(Al,Si)_2O_6 — 4.2\%)$; opaque oxides (1%); uralite $((Ca,Na)_{2-3}(Mg,Fe^{+2},Fe^{+3},Al)_5$ $(Al,Si)_8O_{22}(H)_2 — 0.6\%)$; quartz $(SiO_2 — 0.5\%)$; olivine $((Mg,Fe)_2SiO_4 — trace)$; biotite $K(Mg,Fe)_3(Al,Si_3O_{10})$ (OH)— trace) (Davidson, *in* Sims and Morey, 1972, p. 356). These minerals appear to have been segregated at depth from other minerals of the Duluth Complex. They then appear to have been injected into the surrounding diabase as a crystalline mush (Sims and Morey, *in* Sims and Morey, 1972, p. 12).

Anorthosite has been used for building stone, riprap, and roof-surfacing material. The fountain on the waterfront at Grand Marais and the Grand Marais ranger station are both made from anorthosite.

7

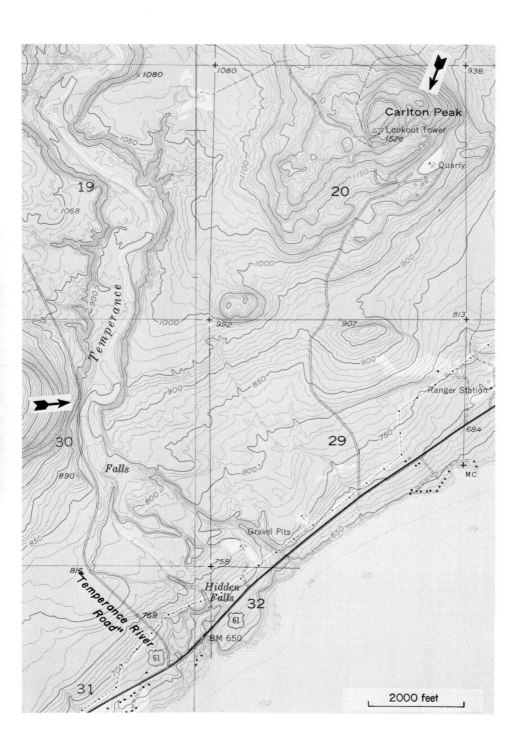

19

20

Carlton Peak

Lookout Tower
1526

Quarry

x1080

1080

938

1080

1050

1000

1150

1100

x1068

900

1000

Temperance

1000

992

907

813

30

900

900

850

Ranger Station

Falls

800

750

684

890

800

29

MC

850

800

650

119

50

816

758

102

Temperance River Road

769

Hidden Falls

32

61

Gravel Pits

703

61

BM 650

31

2000 feet

View of Carlton Peak, a large anorthosite knob near Tofte.

8 Lake Superior Beaches

Cook County

COUNTY: **Cook**
NEAREST TOWN: **Hovland**
OWNERSHIP: **State of Minnesota**
USGS TOPOGRAPHIC MAPS: **Kadunce River, 7½′, 1960; Marr Island, 7½′, 1960**

Lake Superior is bound not only by high rock headlands and shelving rock shores but also by stretches of beach—boulders, cobbles, pebbles, and occasionally sand. Beaches have formed not only along the present-day shore but also along the shores of the past. Abandoned beach ridges, remnants of older strands, are seen high above the present lake. These elevated beaches are the mark of Lake Superior's glacial ancestors. Particularly noteworthy among these beaches are those in eastern Cook County between Croftville and Hovland, near the mouths of the Kadunce and Brule rivers. The shore in this vicinity is gently sloping, has an abundance of loose debris, and is subject to storm wave action—ideal for the study of beach development, for strolling, and for wading.

An interesting walk following a modern-day beach backed by older beaches begins 1.5 miles east of the Kadunce River, approximately 10 miles east of Grand Marais. Park alongside U.S. Highway 61 near Lake Superior. Walk eastward along the shore for approximately one mile. Return along the beach or along the highway. This beach route crosses several low rock points and leads into a small, quiet cove. Storm ridges are seen along this beach. A small rock island connected to the shore by a tombolo, or narrow gravel bar, may also be seen along the beach. Children as well as adults will enjoy this outing. There are innumerable skipping stones, rocks of many kinds, raspberries and thimbleberries in season, clear but terribly cold swimming water, and beautiful picnic spots.

Beaches are the principal product of shore deposition on Lake Superior. They have been cut into the soft amygdaloidal tops of Precambrian basalt flows and into old glacial lake and ice-deposited sediments. They have blocked the mouths of many streams where water is shallow and debris abundant. They usually consist of rock but occasionally consist of sand. They are forming today and have formed in the past; they run along the present lake and high above it. Near the Kadunce River there are many abandoned beaches—20, 30, 40, and 50 feet above the present lake. These are from an earlier, higher glacial stage of Lake Superior called Lake Nipissing. They formed approximately 3500 years ago. Farther inland there are older, less pronounced beaches approximately 440 and 660 feet above the present lake (Grout, Sharp, and Schwartz, 1959, p. 73). These beaches are from yet earlier and higher glacial stages of Lake Superior—Lakes Algonquin and Duluth.

The present-day beach in this vicinity consists of flat rocks and stones of red felsite, gray basalt, and speckled granite. There are also smaller-sized pebbles of agate and jasper. Such flat-pebble beaches are common along Lake Superior. They result from backwash rolling away the rounded rocks and leaving the flattened rocks: the flattened rocks do not roll, they simply slide and resist. All shapes and sizes of rocks wash up on the beach, but only selected ones remain. These flat-pebble beaches, like other beaches, are in constant flux. The stones and the finer materials move back and forth across and down along the beach, powered by waves, backwash, and shore currents. Large storm waves take the smaller materials out into the lake and pile the larger materials into parallel ridges on the shore. Storm ridges are particularly evident on this beach.

The beaches here, typical of many

beaches along Lake Superior, have formed in coves separated by rocky points. The coves form in less resistant rock. The more resistant rock forms the intervening points. This serrate pattern of sharp points and cuspate coves is expressed only in a limited manner near the Kadunce River. It is, however, far more pronounced several miles to the east, beyond the Brule River. The pattern exists on a grand scale near the Baptism River (Site #6).

Older and higher beaches may also be seen along this section of the coast. Walk into the brush and woods behind the present-day beach. The ground rises and falls in a regular manner. The ridges are abandoned beaches and indicate past lake levels. These beach ridges, although only a few feet high, produced a marked variation in vegetation: they support mountain ash, paper birch, bunchberry, and bluebead lily. The intervening swales support yellow birch, spruce, and alder. Occasionally the swales are very wet, consisting of spruce swamp and sphagnum bog. Many of these beach ridges can be traced for miles, occasionally replaced by wave-cut cliffs.

These old shorelines have been mapped, tracing the postglacial history of the Lake Superior basin. The beaches have recorded changing water levels. Their gentle rise to the north has recorded changing land levels. Since glacial retreat the water has dropped and the land has risen.

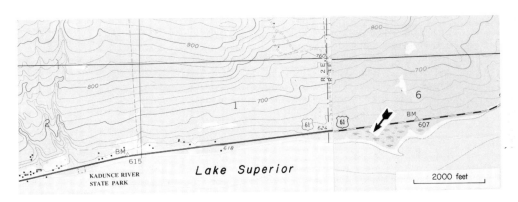

(Site #8)

Flat pebbles on Lake Superior beach.

Lake Superior and crescent-shaped beach with storm ridges.

9 Grand Portage Highlands

Wauswaugoning Bay Overlook, Cook County

COUNTY: **Cook**
NEAREST TOWN: **Grand Portage**
OWNERSHIP: **Public roadway and Indian reservation**
USGS TOPOGRAPHIC MAP: **Grand Portage, 7½′, 1959**

Near Grand Portage are rugged rock ridges and gentle marshy lowlands, sheer bluffs and shallow bays—the Grand Portage highlands. This is a dramatic and striking landscape, produced through the differential erosion of Precambrian rock. Over millions of years, stream erosion and glacial scour have removed proportionately more of the soft than the hard rock, leaving a local relief of greater than 600 feet. The ridges have formed on a dark, resistant rock named diabase. The lowlands and bays have formed in softer slate and sandstone. U.S. Highway 61 and a multitude of hiking trails cross this highland region. From the Wauswaugoning Bay Overlook may be seen mountainous ridges, shallow bays, and low islands. Far out in Lake Superior may be seen high, rock-ridged Isle Royale.

The Wauswaugoning Bay Overlook is located along U.S. Highway 61, approximately three miles north of Grand Portage Village, one-quarter mile beyond Mount Josephine. Highway signs mark both Mount Josephine and the overlook. There is a parking area and restroom at the overlook. Northeast of the overlook are Pigeon Point and the Susie Islands; southeast are Mount Josephine and Hat Point.

Across the highway, between the overlook and Mount Josephine, is an overgrown turnout. Teal Lake and the mountainous country to the northwest may be seen from there. Views in all directions are available from the crest of Mount Josephine.

The Rove slate (Rove Formation), formed from the mud of a Precambrian sea, underlies most of this region. The dark "blackboard rock" may be examined in the road cut along U.S. Highway 61, approximately one mile north of the overlook. After consolidation, the rock was slightly tilted to the southeast and was intruded by molten diabase. This diabase cuts both across and between the layers of slate, producing dikes and sills. The northwest-southeast trending ridges are dikes. They cut across the layers of slate. The northeast-southwest trending ridges, parallel to the slate beds, are sills. This dike-and-sill pattern is very pronounced here in the Grand Portage highlands. Hat Point, a dike, culminates in Mount Josephine, 746 feet above Lake Superior. The steep ridge paralleling U.S. Highway 61 is a sill, which extends northeast to produce Pigeon Falls on the Pigeon River. Pigeon Point is also a sill.

The Pigeon Point sill extends for six miles into Lake Superior and consists not only of diabase but also of gabbro and granite. The variety and layering of these rocks have not only made this sill resistant to erosion, but have also made it a classic spot for geologic inquiry. What is the exact origin of these rocks and how are they related to one another? It is currently believed that the molten mass forming these rocks cooled underground and the various minerals became segregated through gravity separation. Some contamination of the molten material seems also to have occurred at its contact with the surrounding rock.

From this overlook will also be seen the Susie Islands and the abandoned shorelines of Lake Superior's glacial ancestors. The low-lying Susie Islands, often fog wrapped, rugged, rocky, and isolated, consist of slate, sandstone, and basalt. There are small abandoned copper mines on the islands. Part of this archipelago is owned by The Nature Conservancy as a preserve for various tundra plants, far northern plants which grew on these islands during glacial times and continue to thrive here in the harsh conditions of the island's gravel shores. Shorelines of Lake Superior's glacial ancestors are seen as thinly wooded lines paralleling the present-day shore.

There are several excellent trails which lead to further exploration of this highland region. Grand Portage starts at the Grand Portage Outpost and ends nine miles away on the Pigeon River, at the site of old Fort Charlotte. This trail, the historic link between the border lakes and the Great Lakes, avoided the impassable rapids, falls, and rock gorges of the lower Pigeon River. A second and far shorter hike begins near the Grand Portage Outpost and climbs to the top of Mount Rose. This is a nature trail with an accompanying brochure and signs. A third trail climbs to the top of Mount Josephine and out along Hat Point. This trail may be reached either from U.S. Highway 61 or from a gravel pit north of the Grand Portage Outpost. All of these hikes are at least moderately strenuous. They all serve as excellent excursions into the lowlands and onto the mountains and ridges of this striking region.

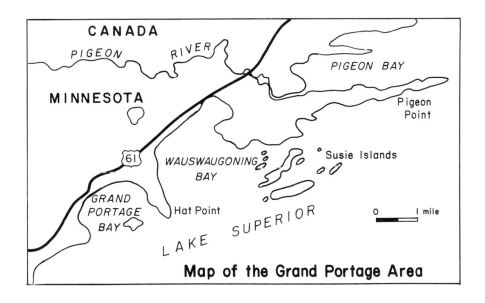

Map of the Grand Portage Area

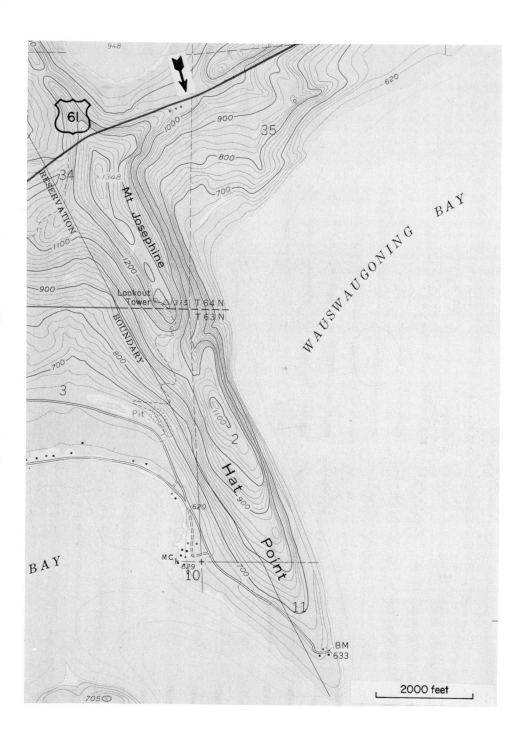

Mount Josephine and Hat Point from the Wauswaugoning Bay Overlook. This mountain and point are formed from a large, resistant diabase dike. The bay has been cut into the surrounding and softer Precambrian sediments.

10　Border Lakes I

Gunflint Lake Overlook, Cook County

COUNTY: **Cook**
NEAREST TOWN: **Grand Marais**
OWNERSHIP: **U.S. Government**
USGS TOPOGRAPHIC MAPS: **Gunflint Lake, 7½', 1960; Long Island Lake, 7½', 1960**

Minnesota's border lakes have formed in basins of Precambrian rock—basins formed through stream erosion and glacial scour. Their underlying bedrock varies in composition and structure, and the shapes of the border lakes reflect this variation. Elongate lakes have formed in soft sediments and along faults. The more irregular lakes have formed in hard homogenous bedrock. Long, linear Gunflint Lake lies within tilted beds of the relatively soft Rove Formation. Neighboring Magnetic Lake lies within the massive Gunflint Iron Formation. Both of these lakes may be seen from the Gunflint Lake Overlook, a spectacular vantage point at the top of a 200-foot cliff.

Gunflint Lake Overlook is between Loon and Gunflint lakes, east of the Gunflint Trail. The overlook is approximately 45 miles from Grand Marais. Turn eastward off the Gunflint Trail to the Loon Lake landing. Proceed one-third mile and park where indicated. Walk down to the landing, and along its far side find a forest trail marked by blue, diamond-shaped signs. Follow this trail to the Gunflint Lake Overlook. The trail begins by running northwest along the base of a low diabase cliff. It climbs fairly steeply, but is relatively easy and short. Its total length is approximately three-quarters mile, and its elevation gain is approximately 200 feet. A leisurely hike up the trail should take about 20 minutes.

The hike to the overlook begins in a small valley. The dominant vegetation is mountain maple and paper birch. Balsam fir and white spruce are also present. In the spring, yellow marsh marigolds bloom along the small bordering stream; late in the summer, the berries of the bluebead lily (*Clintonia borealis*) decorate the pathway.

The trail forks approximately halfway to the overlook. Follow the sign and right-hand fork to the "south rim." The trail continues to climb for a short distance, then levels off in a forest of jack pine. Approximately one-quarter mile from the fork is a "cliffs" sign. The cliffs begin immediately behind this sign, come as a surprise, and are very dangerous. *Do not let children run ahead.*

From the cliffs, the Gunflint Lake Overlook, may be seen both Canada and the United States, the west end of elongate Gunflint Lake, and all of irregular Magnetic Lake. Elongate Gunflint and Loon lakes are typical of lakes in the Rove Formation. Irregular Magnetic Lake is typical of lakes formed in the more uniformly resistant rocks of the Gunflint Iron Formation, Duluth Gabbro, and various granites of the Saganaga, Vermilion, and Snowbank batholiths.

The trail continues eastward along the cliffs, but becomes progressively more poorly marked and more overgrown. Do not follow it and expect to circle back to the Loon Lake landing.

Minnesota's border lake country covers an area of approximately 130 miles east-west by 25 miles north-south. The lakes' varying configurations depend on the underlying bedrock structure and composition. In the eastern one-third of the region, traversed by the Gunflint Trail, there are several distinct lake patterns. To the northeast the lakes are linear and trend east-west—they have formed in the weak, south-dipping Rove Formation. Streams carved valleys within these soft rocks, which were later enlarged and deepened by the scouring of glacial ice and finally filled with water. The ridges between the valleys, now lakes, have formed on resistant sills of diabase. Gunflint and Loon lakes are examples of this lake type. South of the Rove Formation, the lakes are also linear east-west, but they are shallower and more symmetrical. They have been localized in weak zones paralleling the layers of the underlying Duluth Gabbro (Wright, *in* Sims and Morey, 1972, p. 561). At the end of the Gunflint Trail is an area of irregular lakes, epitomized by Lakes Saganaga and Sea Gull (see Site #11). These lake basins have formed in the granitic Saganaga Tonalite.

Southwest of Lake Saganaga—near Cypress, Knife, and Moose lakes—the lakes again exhibit a strong linear pat-

tern. The pattern this time is due to the numerous faults and dikes which cut across various metamorphic rocks. Far to the west, north of Lake Vermilion, are other large, irregular lakes, like Saganaga and Sea Gull, formed in massive granitic rock.

The variation in bedrock structure and composition, and thus lake configuration, has made the canoe country diverse and scenic. Scour by streams and glaciers has produced a unique landscape of lakes, ridges, and hills—a region of half water and half land, a region of diverse geomorphic environments supporting distinct biologic communities. These natural features have combined to make a very special wilderness.

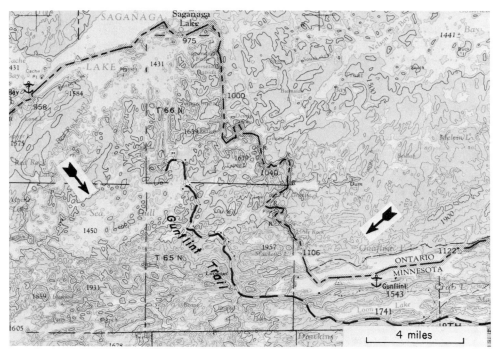

Varying lake configurations due to varying bedrock at the north end of the Gunflint Trail, from the USGS Quetico 1:250,000, 1957 map.

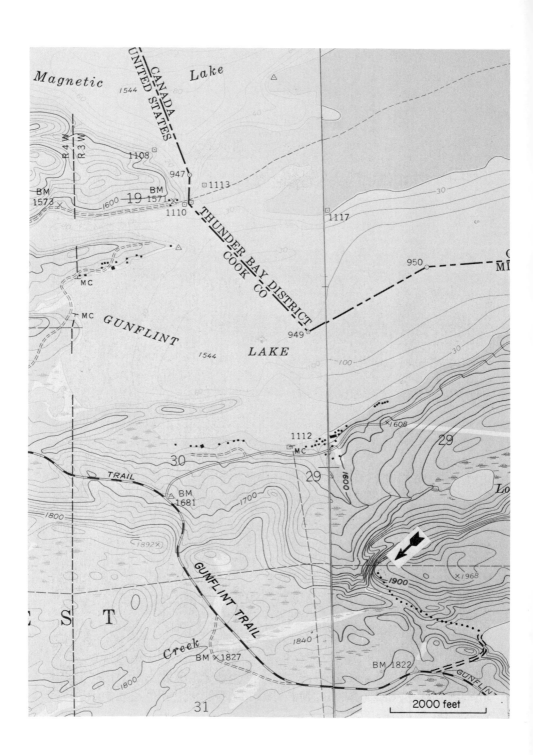

Gunflint Lake Overlook and the west end of Gunflint Lake.

11 Border Lakes II

Sea Gull Lake, Cook County

COUNTY: **Cook**
NEAREST TOWN: **Grand Marais**
OWNERSHIP: **U.S. Government**
USGS TOPOGRAPHIC MAP: **Munker Island, 7½′, 1959**

Sea Gull Lake is large, irregular, and island studded (see small scale map, Site #10). It is typical of the granitic-basined lakes of the Boundary Waters Canoe Area (BWCA). Its configuration results from glacial scour of a massive, relatively uniform rock, the Saganaga Tonalite. This particular rock also underlies Lake Saganaga, hence its name. The border canoeist finds these granitic lakes perhaps the loveliest and certainly the most confusing in his or her travels. They are variously flanked by steep rock cliffs, high rounded hills, long sloping points, and deep rock-bound or marsh-fringed bays. They are filled with a multitude of islands—large and small, wooded and barren—islands which appear suddenly from unknown depths or rise gradually from rocky shoals.

Most of these lakes and their granitic country are accessible only by canoe. However, a small northern bay of Sea Gull Lake may be seen from Trail's End Campground, located on a granitic knob between Sea Gull and Gull lakes. Trail's End Campground is at the end of the Gunflint Trail, approximately 58 miles northwest of Grand Marais. Park near the access to Gull Lake, then walk counterclockwise through the campground. Follow along the edge of Gull Lake, the Sea Gull River, and Sea Gull Lake. Note the irregular landscape of rock and water.

This scoured, irregular landscape is typical of the granitic border lakes—the points and cliffs, the lakes and cascades. However, the land surface here is better exposed than in most other places: the Roy Lake fire of 1976 burned off the obscuring vegetation.

The exposed gray-to-pink, medium-to coarse-grained rock is the Saganaga Tonalite, an intrusive igneous rock very similar to granite. It contains large amounts of feldspar and quartz and lesser amounts of hornblende, biotite, chlorite, epidote, and sphene. It is a hard, homogeneous rock, broken only by minor joints and faults. These rock characteristics have led to the irregular lakes and hills. The Saganaga Tonalite surrounds Saganaga, Sea Gull, Mowe, and Northern Light lakes, covering an area of approximately 300 square miles. Similar granitic rock underlies Snowbank, Basswood, LaCroix, and northern Burntside lakes.

Lakes Sea Gull, Gull, and Saganaga are popular starting points for canoe trips. Lake Saganaga is frequently the second most popular starting point for all canoe trips in the BWCA; Sea Gull Lake is the sixth most popular. Indeed, a canoe is the best way to see and to understand the geologic and configurational complexity of the border lakes. Rental canoes are available from the several resorts at this northern end of the Gunflint Trail. Consider renting one for a day or a week—become immersed in rock, water, and wilderness.

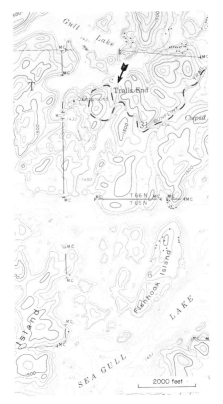

Saganaga Tonalite at Trails End Campground

12 Ely Greenstone

Ely

COUNTY: **St. Louis**
NEAREST TOWN: **Ely**
OWNERSHIP: **Public roadway; outcrop fenced by Ely Rock and Mineral Club, view from public roadway**
USGS TOPOGRAPHIC MAPS: **Shagawa Lake, 7½', 1965; Ely, 7½', 1965**

Greenstones are highly controversial. These Archean rocks generally occur in long, narrow belts surrounded by similarly ancient granites and gneisses. One of these greenstone belts runs through Ely, the rocks cropping out in the streets and on the surrounding hills and ridges. Greenstones are altered, ancient, underwater lava flows. Little more, however, is known about them. Why are they common only in Archean terrane? Why, as many geologists believe, are there no good modern analogues?

Although greenstone exposures are common throughout Ely, two are particularly noteworthy. The first is a road cut immediately west of town. The second is a small rounded rock mass in the northeastern part of town.

Several large road cuts occur along Minnesota Highway 1-169 immediately west of Ely. Examine the westernmost of these, located on the south side of the highway three quarters of a mile west of town. This exposure of Ely Greenstone is 20 to 30 feet high and several hundred feet long. Its typical gray-green color is indicative of its high chlorite and actinolite content. The smooth upper surface of this road cut and outcrop shows glacial striations, thin scratches demonstrating that glaciers once moved over this region.

The second exposure is a small knob eight feet high and 10 to 15 feet across. It is found on the north side of Main Street between Twelfth and Thirteenth avenues east. Main Street is four blocks north of Minnesota Highway 169. This rock knob has been fenced and identified by the Mesabi Rock and Mineral Club. Large ellipsoidal structures called pillows are particularly evident at this location. These pillows, up to several feet across, form when lava cools and solidifies under water. They are typical of Archean greenstones.

Much of the Ely Greenstone, like other Archean greenstones, is a metamorphosed pillow basalt, a dark, fine-grained lava which cooled under water and long after solidification was subjected to heat and pressure. Its gray-green color is imparted primarily by the green metamorphic mineral chlorite, but also by green amphibole and epidote (Sims, *in* Sims and Morey, 1972, p. 63).

The Ely Greenstone belt is almost 40 miles long and two to six miles wide. It runs from Lake Vermilion eastward to near Snowbank Lake. Its exposed thickness is 20,000 feet (Ibid.). It has been dated at 2.6 billion years (Goldich, *in* Sims and Morey, 1972, p. 33) and is similar in age to the nearby gneissic and granitic rocks—the Saganaga Tonalite (see Site #11), the Giants Range Granite (see Site #17), and the Vermilion Granitic Complex.

Why are greenstones so common in Archean rocks? Why are they rarely, if ever, present in younger rocks? Why are there no good modern analogues? Geologists currently believe that greenstone-type pillow basalts form along the boundaries of shifting crustal plates, that is, at zones of weakness where molten material rises upward from the earth's interior and spreads out on the ocean floor. These zones do exist today, places of volcanism, earthquakes, high heat flow, and great crustal instability. But no greenstone exists there. Why not?

Geologists speculate that the earth's heat flow was far greater in the Archean than it is today. Perhaps the earth's crust then was thinner and more

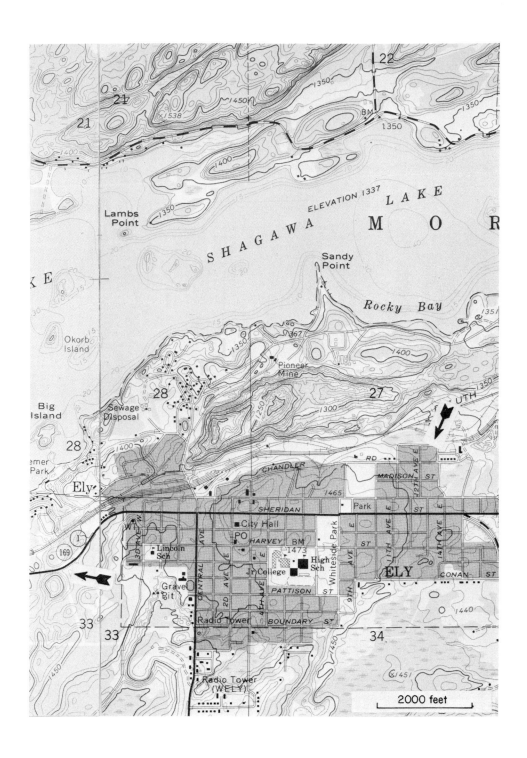

mobile. Were there then more and longer zones of crustal weakness? Was metamorophism almost ubiquitous? As a result, were the rocks at these zones different compositionally from those in the more limited but similar zones of today? None of these questions has been answered to complete satisfaction.

The world's greenstone belts, besides being geologic curiosities, contain a multitude of economic minerals. They are major depositories of gold, silver, chromium, nickel, copper, and zinc (Windley, 1977, p. 37). The Ely rocks are no exception, although the mineral in this instance is iron. An isolated body of iron ore occurs in the upper portion of the Ely Greenstone. This body, or lens, is centered on Ely and is approximately one and three-quarters mile long and a maximum of one-quarter mile wide. The mines in this ore body are recognized by their abandoned pits, shafts, and tailings.

Huge drill cores of the Ely Greenstone, taken in 1938 from Ely's Zenith Mine, are on display at the Minnesota Museum of Mining in Chisholm and at the Department of Geology and Geophysics, University of Minnesota, Minneapolis. These are the world's largest drill cores, five and one-half feet across. The Chisholm core is 12 feet high and weighs 24 tons. Today, many more drill cores are being taken from the world's greenstone belts in a search for answers to the geologic question *why* and the economic question *where*.

Road cut in Ely Greenstone.

Fenced outcrop of Ely Greenstone, Ely. Note the pillow structure.

13 Vermilion Fault

St. Louis County

COUNTY: **St. Louis**
NEAREST TOWN: **Ely**
OWNERSHIP: **Public roadway**
USGS TOPOGRAPHIC MAPS: **Shagawa Lake,
7½', 1965; Ely, 7½', 1965**

The Precambrian rocks of northern
Minnesota have been cut by many large
faults—planes along which the rocks
have split, broken, and moved. The
Vermilion fault is the largest of these
large Precambrian faults. It is com-
parable in length to the great faults of
Canada's Yellowknife district and to the
Great Glen fault of Scotland (Sims, *in*
Sims and Morey, 1972, p. 46). It runs
for more than 250 miles, entering
Northwestern Minnesota near the Red
River, bending southeastward in an ar-
cuate path, and leaving Northeastern
Minnesota near Basswood Lake (see
Bedrock Geology Map). Its surface expression is usually a narrow, linear
topographic depression (Ibid.), occasionally occupied by deep, elongate
lakes.

The Vermilion fault may be seen north
of Ely where it crosses the Echo Trail,
St. Louis County Road 116. From Ely
follow Minnesota Highway 169 east for
approximately one mile. Turn north on
St. Louis County Road 88 and proceed
for 2.2 miles, past Shagawa Lake. Turn
right onto the Echo Trail and proceed
3.2 miles past Shig-Wauk Lodge on Little Long Lake to St. Louis County
Road 752, Moat's Resort Road. This
road and the paralleling power line are
built in and along the Vermilion fault:
note the 50-foot-high ridges on either
side. This valley is a natural feature,
despite the road, powerline, cut vegetation, and its generally artificial appearance. The valley is caused by the
more rapid weathering and erosion of
the crushed rock within the fault zone,
here approximately 200 feet wide. The
fault separates the Vermilion Granite to
the north from the Newton Lake Formation to the south.

Rocks break and move along faults
because of great pressures within the
earth: land masses and ocean basins
shift past one another; molten rock
material rises within the earth's crust,
forcing aside and breaking nearby rock.
The movement along these fractures or
faults may be parallel to the fault,
perpendicular to the fault, or a combination of both. If the movement is
primarily parallel to the plane, or
strike, of the fracture, then it is known
as a strike-slip fault. If the movement is
primarily perpendicular to the strike of
the fault, along the dip, the fault is
known as a dip-slip fault.

The Vermilion fault is a strike-slip
fault. The Red Wing fault (see Site #19)
is a dip-slip fault. The direction and
amount of displacement along the Vermilion fault is not precisely known.
However, the horizontal component is
believed to be several miles and the
vertical component approximately one
mile (Ojakangas and Morey, 1972, p.
18). In contrast, the displacement on the
Red Wing fault is approximately 150
feet.

One of the world's best-known faults
is the San Andreas of California. Like
the Vermilion, it is a major strike-slip
fault. But unlike the Vermilion, it is active at the present time. Californians
live in potential danger from movements
or earthquakes along this giant fault.

Minnesota has numerous other faults
(snow, mosquitoes, . . .); however,
most of Minnesota's faults are confined
to the Precambrian terrane of northern
Minnesota. None of these faults is active, and most have been inactive for
hundreds of millions or even billions of
years. Thus the destruction of San Francisco by movement along the San Andreas fault would be devastating but an-
ticipated; the destruction of Ely by
movement along the Vermilion fault
would be a complete geologic surprise.

Narrow, steep-sided valley, the topographic expression of the Vermilion fault, along the Echo Trail.

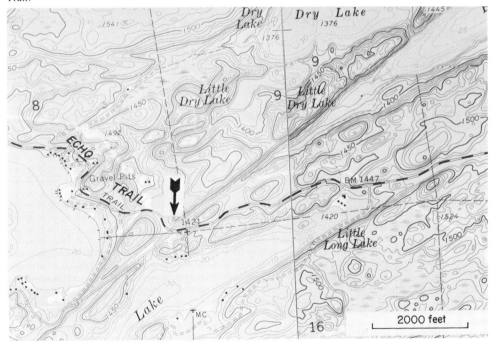

14 Soudan Iron Formation

Soudan Hill, Tower-Soudan State Park

COUNTY: **St. Louis**
NEAREST TOWN: **Soudan**
OWNERSHIP: **State of Minnesota**
USGS TOPOGRAPHIC MAP: **Soudan, 7½',**
1956

The Soudan Iron Formation is the largest iron-formation in the Vermilion district. The Vermilion district is a belt of metamorphosed volcanic and sedimentary rock which is bordered by granitic rocks of the Giants Range batholith to the south, the Vermilion batholith to the north, and the Saganaga batholith to the east (Sims and Morey, *in* Sims and Morey, 1972, p. 6). This formation consists of conspicuously banded iron-bearing chert interbedded with tuff, agglomerate, and basalt (Ojakangas and Morey, 1972, p. 7). It is named for exposures on Soudan Hill, site of Minnesota's oldest and deepest mine, the Soudan Mine. Visitors may climb Soudan Hill. They may also enter the underground mine, ride an elevator nearly one-half mile below the earth's surface, and examine the rocks and workings of a particular ore body. Both the hill and mine are found within Tower-Soudan State Park.

Tower-Soudan State Park is located immediately north of Soudan and south of Lake Vermilion. Follow Minnesota Highway 1-169 to the west side of Soudan. Turn north on St. Louis County Road 697 and proceed approximately one-half mile to the park entrance. The park encompasses 982 acres and is open year-round. Underground mine tours are conducted May 18 through Labor Day. Camping is available at nearby Bear Head State Park on Bear Head Lake or McKinley Park on Lake Vermilion. For further information write: Superintendent, Tower-Soudan State Park, Tower, Minnesota 55790.

The Soudan Mine has been dug into the rich ores of the Soudan Iron Formation. Minnesota's iron mining industry was born here, and the mine's opening in 1884 was one of the great commercial events of the nineteenth century. The mine began as an open-pit operation, but quickly moved underground. It was in almost continuous operation from 1884 to 1962, when U.S. Steel donated this mine to the state of Minnesota. Interestingly, the mine was not closed because of the exhaustion of the ore, but because of the high cost of mining it and the preference for blast furnaces and the lower-grade pelletized taconite (Ibid., p. 30).

The Soudan Iron Formation of the Vermilion Iron Range is unlike that of the Biwabik Iron Formation of the Mesabi Iron Range. The Soudan Iron Formation consists of isolated pockets of iron-bearing rock, which are intricately folded, of little lateral extent, and extend to great depth. The dominant ore variety, jaspilite, is a strikingly banded red, white, silver-gray, and black rock made of thin, alternating laters of jasper, quartz, chert, and hematite. The ore-bearing rocks of the Mesabi Iron Range are of great lateral extent, extend to little depth, and are dominantly a soft, red, earthy hematite. The Mesabi ores lie just below the surface and can be mined by open-pit methods; the Vermilion ores must be mined through underground shafts.

Besides jaspilite, there are other iron-bearing rocks within the Soudan Iron Formation—red hematite, greenish white chert, and green jasper. Ore sought within the mine is a hard, bluish hematite (Fe_2O_3), a very high-grade ore consisting of 65% iron. The jaspilite and other ores may be seen within the mine and on the mine dump near the parking lot. A huge chunk of jaspilite is on display in the small park on the south side of Soudan, along the north side of Minnesota Highway 1-169.

The Soudan Iron Formation overlies the mafic volcanic rocks of the Ely Greenstone (Site #12) and in turn is overlain by the clastic rocks of the Vermilion Formation (Sims, *in* Sims and Morey, 1972, p. 79). Close association of the iron-formation with the volcanic rocks suggests a volcanic source for their chemical components. Perhaps these volcanic sediments, along with local concentrations of silicon dioxide, accumulated in shallow marine basins. Long after solidification and compaction, the lean ores changed to high-grade ores: circulating waters removed the silicon dioxide and concentrated the iron.

The answers are far from in on the origin of the Soudan and other Precambrian iron-formations. Most of the world's major iron-formations formed during the Precambrian, between 1.7 and 2.2 billion years ago. Why? Perhaps a different type of atmosphere existed then; perhaps the oceans contained more dissolved iron and silica than today; perhaps primitive algae releasing oxygen concentrated the excess iron.

The Soudan Iron Formation has been mined for nearly a century, and a great deal is known about its occurrence and mineralogy. The iron has immeasurably affected the region's history and economic development. The exact origin of the ore, however, remains a mystery.

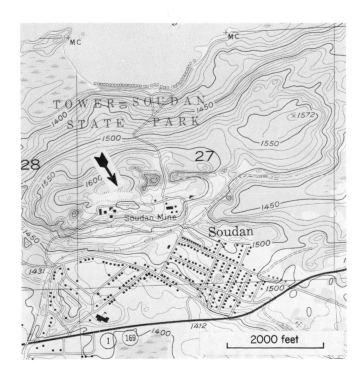

Close-up of jaspilite, an ore-bearing rock of the Soudan Formation.

Mesabi Iron Range

Iron Range Interpretive Center, Chisholm

COUNTY: **St. Louis**
NEAREST TOWN: **Chisholm**
OWNERSHIP: **State of Minnesota**
USGS TOPOGRAPHIC MAP: **Hibbing, 7½',
1957**

The Iron Range Interpretive Center near
Chisholm is an essential stop on any
geologic tour of Minnesota. It is located
in the heart of the Mesabi Iron Range
and sits on the north side of the abandoned Glen Mine. In the center are
numerous displays and recordings concerning the geologic and human history
of Minnesota's iron ranges. Near the
center are nature trails and a picnic
area.

The Iron Range Interpretive Center is
located approximately three-quarter mile
south of Chisholm on the east side of
Minnesota Highway 169. Follow the
signs to an attractive, low white
building. The center's summer hours,
between Memorial and Labor days, are
9 a.m. to 9 p.m.; the winter hours are
9 a.m. to 5 p.m. The admission charge
for adults is $1.50, for people under
17, $ .50. For more information you
may write or call: The Iron Range Interpretive Center, Box 392, Chisholm,
Minnesota 55719. Phone: (218)
254-3323.

Iron is the fourth most common element
in the earth's crust, following oxygen,
silicon, and aluminum. Five percent of
the earth's crust is made up of iron.
Iron occurs in many kinds of rock;
however, its ores are concentrated only
occasionally and in small and widely
scattered areas. Minnesota's Mesabi
Iron Range is one of the world's
greatest concentrations of iron ore. It is
an irregular streak of iron ore—taconite,

limonite, and hematite—120 miles long
and one to three miles wide. In the late
1940s and 1950s the Mesabi Range con-
sistently produced approximately one
third of the world's iron ore (Schwartz
and Thiel, 1954, p. 244). Today it does
not produce nearly that amount of ore,
but it does account for nearly two thirds
of the United States' total production.
During the 1940s iron from the Hull-
Rust Mine alone accounted for as much
as 10% of the world's total production.
Iron from Minnesota was used to make
most of the steel for the allied armies in
the first and second world wars.

The iron mining industry has attracted
people from more than three dozen
nations—including Norway, Ireland,
Britain, Wales, Yugoslavia, Poland,
Germany, and China. Note all the
foreign flags which fly along the
highway on the shores of Lake
Longyear just east of Chisholm. The
towns of Chisholm, Tower, Eveleth,
Biwabik, and Buhl all owe their existence to the iron-mining industry. The
Lake Superior ports of Duluth,
Superior, Silver Bay, Taconite Harbor,
and Two Harbors all have a significant
portion of their populations involved in
iron-ore shipping. The economy of all
Northeastern Minnesota has fluctuated
from boom to bust, depending on war
and peace, domestic and foreign
markets, and technological advances.

The Biwabik Iron Formation, the
heart of the Mesabi Range, was formed
around one and two billion years ago.
The ore formed at this time is the abundant, hard, low-grade taconite. These
ores were enriched approximately 100
million years ago when water circulating through the rock leached out
silica and left concentrations of iron oxide. This enriched ore is a soft, high-
grade hematite and limonite. The
pockets of high-grade ore, approximately 10% of the formation, have been virtually mined out, and the lower-grade
taconite is currently being mined.

The Biwabik Iron Formation is
believed to have been laid down in a
relatively clear Precambrian sea which

15

contained iron and silicon. Most of the iron from that sea was precipitated in the form of carbonates and silicates, and these minerals became enmeshed in a matrix of very fine-grained silica. The source of the iron and silica is not known. It is also not known exactly why and under what conditions this iron was precipitated. However, it is commonly believed that primitive algae were active contributors to the ore-forming process. Their fossils (some of the world's oldest) are found within the rock, and it is believed that they released oxygen, trapping and concentrating the iron which was dissolved in the seawater. The mass of iron carbonate and silicate minerals lying on the ocean floor later became a rock called ferruginous, or iron-bearing, chert—the bulk of the Biwabik Iron Formation.

Once the Mesabi Iron Range was marked by Mesaba, a legendary, sleeping, red Ojibway giant, and uninterrupted forest. Today it is marked by huge open pits and towering tailing piles. Little vegetation remains on this broken rock. The towns of Virginia, Hibbing, Chisholm, Biwabik, Eveleth, and others replaced the villages of Indian teepees. Today the ore which took over a billion years to form is taking just a hundred years to mine.

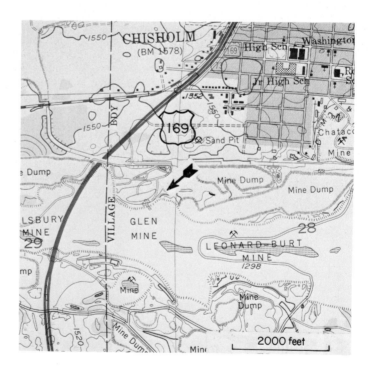

Iron Range Interpretive Center perched on the edge of the Glen Mine, Chisholm.

16 Rouchleau Mine

Mine View in the Sky, Virginia

COUNTY: **St. Louis**
NEAREST TOWN: **Virginia**
OWNERSHIP: **City of Virginia**
USGS TOPOGRAPHIC MAP: **Virginia, 7½',
1951**

There are a number of excellent vantage points for mines on the Mesabi Iron Range. One of the best of these is Mine View in the Sky overlooking the Rouchleau Mine. The view and mine are particularly impressive, since the city of Virginia is perched along the western edge of this large open pit. The city thus gives some visual perspective to this mine, which is nearly three miles long, one-half mile wide, and 450 feet deep. The pit's bottom is partially covered with an ever-changing, sky-reflecting lake. The pit sides expose multi-colored rock layers of orange, purple, black, beige, and gray.

Mine View in the Sky is located one-quarter mile east of Minnesota Highway 135, approximately one-half mile southeast of Virginia. This is near the intersection of U.S. Highway 53 and Minnesota Highway 169. Follow the signs to the entrance road, which winds up a huge mine dump and ends at a parking area and information building. Admission is $1 per car. Near the parking area is a drill core, a drill bit, an ore scoop, and a large slab of taconite—apparently placed here for adult inspection and curious, climbing-minded children. This observation area was built originally as a survey point for the pit foreman. Today visitors can do the same thing: oversee the entire mine area from this one position.

The Rouchleau Mine has been operated by U.S. Steel and its predecessors since

1893. The mine began as a series of underground shafts and later became an open-pit operation. The mine has produced more than 300 million gross tons of both high- and low-grade ore. Today all the ore produced from this mine is a soft hematite-limonite, which after upgrading has an average iron content of 53.7% (Iron Range Resources and Rehabilitation Board brochure "Rouchleau Group").

This mine is in the Biwabik Iron Formation (see Site #15), a rock unit formed from water-lain Precambrian sediments. This formation is made up of red rock, hematite, limonite, chert, and jaspilite, all of which produce the multitude of colors seen in the pit. In this vicinity the formation is basically flat lying or only slightly tilted; however, a large fold appears in the opposite wall of the mine.

Overlying the iron-formation are Cretaceous and glacial sediments—clays, silts, sands, and gravels. Some of these materials produce the gray and beige layers seen high on the pit walls to the north and east.

Mine View in the Sky is only one of numerous vantage points on the Minnesota iron ranges. Other noteworthy viewpoints are found at 1) the Pioneer Mine in Ely, 2) the Longyear Drill Site near Hoyt Lakes, 3) the Grant Mine near Buhl, 4) the Bruce Mine near Chisholm, 5) the Hull-Rust Mine near Hibbing, 6) the Hill Annex Mine near Calumet, 7) the Croft Mine near Crosby, and 8) the Eveleth Mines in Eveleth. For more information write: The Iron Range Resources and Rehabilitation Board, Highway 53 South, P.O. Box 678, Eveleth, Minnesota 55734. Phone: (218) 749-8260.

View of the Rouchleau Mine and city of Virginia, Mine View in the Sky.

(Site #16)

17 Giants Range Batholith

Virginia

COUNTY: **St. Louis**
NEAREST TOWN: **Virginia**
OWNERSHIP: **Public roadway**
USGS TOPOGRAPHIC MAP: **Virginia, 7½',
1951**

A batholith is any body of intrusive rock which covers at least 40 square miles and maintains its diameter or grows larger to unknown depths. The Giants Range batholith is a large, complex body of medium to coarsely crystalline granitic rock. It extends for nearly 200 miles, from Wadena to Ely (Sims and Viswanathan, *in* Sims and Morey, 1972, p. 120) and ranges in width from five to 25 miles (Ojakangas and Morey, 1972, p. 16). Its exposed portion forms the Giants Range, or Ridge, a high rock spine along the northern side of the Mesabi Iron Range. This batholith, like the nearby Vermilion and Saganaga batholiths (Site #11), formed during the Archean, 2.7 billion years ago (Sims and Viswanathan, *in* Sims and Morey, 1972, p. 121). This was a time of intense regional deformation, when the rocks of northern Minnesota were melted, emplaced, and deformed on a large scale.

The variety and complexity of rock types which make up the Giants Range batholith may be seen approximately three miles north of Virginia. There U.S. Highway 53–Minnesota Highway 169 climbs over the Giants Ridge, cutting through the rock at its crest. Park at the wayside east of the highway, below Lookout Mountain. Walk northward to the Laurentian Divide sign (see Site #18). Then walk westward to the highway. Examine the rocks between the sign and the highway, along the east side of the highway, along the west side of the highway, and in the median. Be very careful. This is a dangerous spot, with heavy, fast-moving traffic.

The Giants Range batholith, although primarily granitic, is highly variable in both mineralogy and texture. It is considered to be a typical Algoman (a portion of the Archean) batholith (Ibid., p. 120). It appears to have formed from both the intrusion of molten rock and from the partial melting of preexisting rock. At this single exposure are gray granite gneiss, pink granite, mottled black-and-white diorite, and dark amphibolite. There also appear to be altered basalt flows and volcanic tuffs. In some places these rock types are entirely distinct from one another; in other places the transition is fully gradational. Some rocks seemed to have cooled from a melt; some rocks appear to have been incorporated piecemeal within a melt; some rocks appear to have only partially melted.

Certain rock types appear to exist as isolated fragments entirely surrounded by other rock types, like dates in a pudding. Such a relationship may indicate that the melting points of the two rocks were different and that the "dates" were simply incorporated as solids into a liquid or semiliquid "pudding." This relationship is seen at the southern end of the outcrop along the east side of the highway between the Laurentian Divide sign and the roadway. Irregular fragments of the dark rock amphibolite are surrounded by gray granite gneiss.

Some rocks appear to cut across one another. Younger rocks cut older rocks; molten rocks cut solid rocks. This relationship is seen at the northern end of the outcrop on the east side of the median where a gray granite gneiss is cut by a mottled black-and-white diorite, which in turn is cut by a pink granite. It follows that the granite is younger than the diorite, which in turn is younger than the gneiss.

Many rocks seem simply to phase into one another. This indicates at least partial and often complete melting. This relationship is seen most easily along the west side of the highway, on the south end of the southbound lane.

Another rock relationship exists below the roadside Laurentian Divide sign. There a vertical, variously colored fracture crosses the otherwise gray rocks. This six-inch-wide zone of broken and altered rock is a small fault, a common feature of this batholith.

These observations make it apparent that the Giants Range batholith is indeed a highly complex crystalline rock with a long and varied history. It was formed at a time in the Precambrian when apparently great portions of the earth's crust became molten. Similar granitic batholiths are found throughout Northeastern Minnesota, Canada, and many of the world's other shield areas. The examination of this particular batholith may well throw light on the formation and subsequent history of them all.

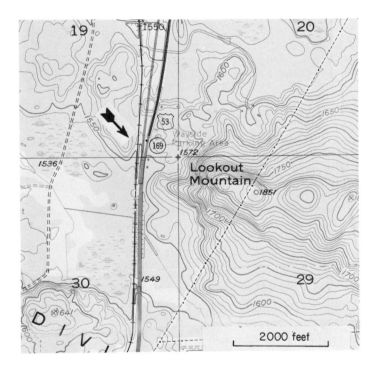

Road cut in the Giants Range batholith.

Close-up of rock in the Giants Range batholith. Dark amphibolite and diorite are cut by thin dikes of lighter colored granite.

Laurentian Divide

St. Louis County

COUNTY: **St. Louis**
NEAREST TOWN: **Virginia**
OWNERSHIP: **U.S. Government**
USGS TOPOGRAPHIC MAP: **Virginia, 7½',**
1951

Any rain shower which falls on North America must sink into the ground, evaporate, or flow away to the north, south, east, or west. In certain places this rain shower must split, with portions of it flowing one way and portions of it flowing another. Such a place of division between river basins is called a watershed or drainage divide. The Laurentian Divide separates the waters going north to the Arctic Ocean and south to the Atlantic Ocean. In Minnesota this divide runs irregularly from Browns Valley, at the headwaters of the Minnesota and Red rivers, to northern Cook County, at the headwaters of the Rainy and Pigeon rivers. An excellent place to see this divide is on the Giants Ridge several miles north of Virginia. There, placed on top of the divide, is a large, colorful National Forest Service sign. This is the same site used for the Giants Range batholith (Site #17).

The Giants Range and the Laurentian Divide is crossed by U.S. Highway 53–Minnesota Highway 169 approximately three miles north of Virginia. Park at the wayside east of the highway on the west flank of Lookout Mountain. In the woods, on the north end of the parking area, is the large Laurentian Divide sign. Read the sign and note that the land does indeed fall away both to the north and to the south.

Minnesota lies at the center of North America and includes the source of three of North America's greatest river systems: the Red River of the North, the Mississippi River, and the St.

Lawrence River. The Red River, flowing northward along Minnesota's western border, empties into Hudson Bay and thence the Arctic Ocean. The Mississippi River and its tributaries, the St. Croix and Minnesota rivers, flow southward and empty into the Gulf of Mexico. The St. Louis River, Baptism River, Gooseberry River, and other North Shore rivers all empty into Lake Superior, which in turn empties into Lakes Michigan and Huron, the lower Great Lakes, the St. Lawrence River, and ultimately the Atlantic Ocean. The Rainy River, flowing westward along most of Minnesota's northern border, ultimately empties into Hudson Bay. The Laurentian Divide thus divides the Red River and Rainy River basins from the Minnesota, Mississippi, and Lake Superior basins (see the Physiographic Map of Minnesota). The divide marks the separation of waters flowing north to the Arctic and south and east to the Atlantic.

In Northeastern Minnesota, north of the Minnesota iron ranges, the Laurentian Divide occupies the crest of a line of low, rugged, Precambrian rock hills known as the Giants Ridge. Farther east, the Laurentian Divide follows the crest of the North Shore highland (see Site #2). In western Minnesota the Laurentian Divide follows the Big Stone, Alexandria, and Itasca moraines, belts of very young glacially-deposited hills.

Eastward from Minnesota the Laurentian Divide wanders off into Canada north of Lakes Superior and Nipigon and eastward through Ontario, Quebec, and Labrador, across the Laurentian highlands. Westward, after leaving Minnesota at Browns Valley, the divide crosses North Dakota and then southern Saskatchewan and Alberta, dividing the Souris and Saskatchewan rivers from the Missouri River. The Laurentian Divide then reaches the Rocky Mountains and joins the continental divide, which runs north-south along their crest and marks the division between rivers flowing west to the Pacific and east to

18

the Gulf of Mexico. Another continental divide follows the crest of the Appalachian Mountains, separating waters that flow east into the Atlantic from those that flow south into the Gulf of Mexico.

North America's major drainage divides have stayed stable over long periods of time. However, large disruptions of drainage have occurred during the Pleistocene, when glacial ice sheets advanced southward over North America. Other disruptions and drainage changes have occurred during the uplift of mountains and plateaus.

Laurentian Divide where it is crossed by U.S. Highway 53–Minnesota Highway 169, several miles north of Virginia. Here the divide runs along the crest of the Giants Range.

Laurentian Divide sign north of Virginia. "The Laurentian Divide is the ridge of low, rugged hills meandering through Northern Minnesota that separates the headwaters of streams which flow North and South. Streams which begin on the North slope of the Divide flow through Canada to Hudson Bay and the Arctic Ocean. On the opposite side of the divide, streams flow South into Lake Superior, eventually reaching the Atlantic Ocean. The Laurentian Divide, at this location, is only a remnant of a once gigantic mountain range formed more than a billion years ago."

Highly dissected landscape typical of the Driftless Area of Southeastern Minnesota.

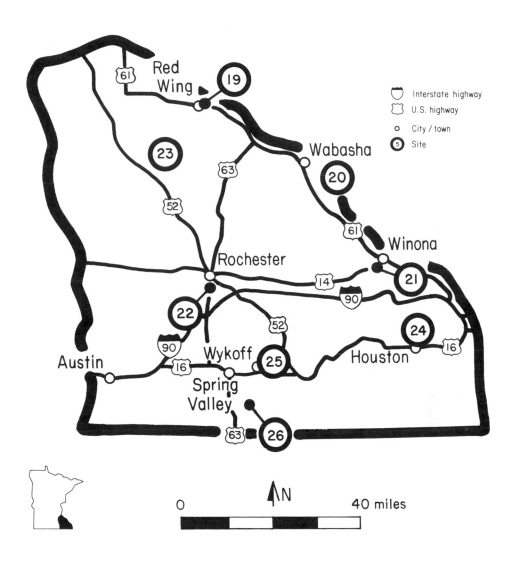

Interstate highway
U.S. highway
City / town
Site

Red Wing
61
19
Wabasha
23
63
20
52
61
Winona
Rochester
14
21
90
22
52
24
90
16
Austin
16
Wykoff
25
Houston
Spring
Valley
63
26

0   40 miles

N

II Southeastern Minnesota

Paleozoic Rocks, Surface Water and Groundwater

Southeastern Minnesota is a land of gently rolling uplands, deep wooded ravines, and large, slow-flowing rivers. Its basic framework is several hundred feet of flat-lying Paleozoic rock, overlain in places by glacial debris and everywhere cut by surface water and groundwater.

The region is bounded on the west by a belt of hills, marking the edge of Minnesota's most recent glaciation. The hills run southward from Lakeville through Faribault, Waseca, and Albert Lea to the Iowa border. On the north the region is bounded by the young glacial deposits of the Twin Cities metropolitan area. It is bounded on the east by the Mississippi River and on the south by Iowa.

Encountered only in the deepest wells of southeastern Minnesota are Precambrian rocks, ancient rocks similar in age to those along the North Shore. Virtually all rocks exposed at the surface are of Paleozoic age, 350 to 600 million years old. Represented in the Mississippi River bluffs alone are more than 150 million years of geologic history. These rocks record the advance and retreat of shallow semitropical seas.

The rocks, originally laid flat, remain that way. They have only occasionally been displaced by faulting, fracturing due to shearing forces deep within the earth's crust, and broad warping. They have never been turned, twisted, or melted.

After the Paleozoic seas retreated, the land was subject to erosion by wind and water for more than 300 million years. Dinosaurs fed in lush swamps and forests. Horsetails and ferns were replaced by flowering plants. Ancestors of the rhinoceros and antelope ran across grassy plains, yet in

Minnesota no record remains of these things; wind and water carried away the evidence.

Approximately two million years ago, the earth's climate changed. Glaciers covered much of the Northern Hemisphere, advancing over Minnesota four separate times. The early glaciations covered the northern portions of Southeastern Minnesota. The most recent glaciation, the Wisconsin, did not. The area south and west of Winona may never have been covered by glacial ice.

As the glaciers melted they dropped their load of clays, silts, sands, and rocks. Seventy-five to 100 feet of this debris forms the high, gently rolling plains between Zumbrota and Rochester. The melting ice also released a tremendous volume of water, which enlarged ancient drainageways and carved new ones. Thus Southeastern Minnesota, even though not always covered by glacial ice, felt its impact. The Cannon, Zumbro, Whitewater, and Root rivers grew unbelievably. They cut enormous valleys and flowed swiftly into a far larger Mississippi River, a river often four miles across.

Not only have surface waters sculptured the land, but so also have groundwaters. The weak carbonic acid formed by rain water and carbon dioxide has slowly dissolved surface limestone, leaving cavities, caverns, caves, and sinks. Fillmore County is dotted with sinks, holes in the ground, into which surface streams flow and disappear.

Even today the surface waters and groundwaters continue inexorably to erode and dissolve the rock, narrowing the divides and enlarging the valleys of this highly picturesque region.

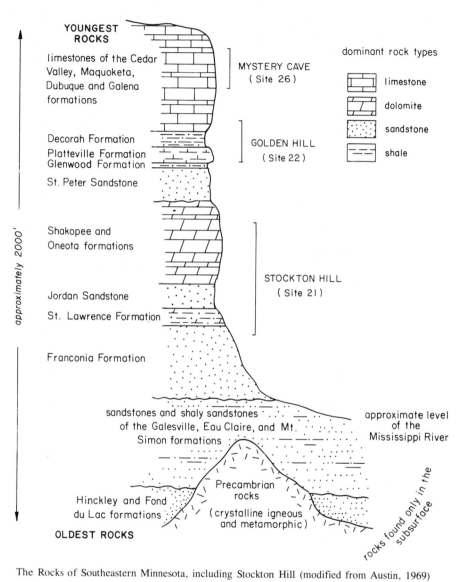

YOUNGEST
ROCKS

limestones of the Cedar
Valley, Maquoketa,
Dubuque and Galena
formations

MYSTERY CAVE
(Site 26)

Decorah Formation
Platteville Formation
Glenwood Formation

St. Peter Sandstone

GOLDEN HILL
(Site 22)

dominant rock types

limestone

dolomite

sandstone

shale

approximately 2000'

Shakopee and
Oneota formations

STOCKTON HILL
(Site 21)

Jordan Sandstone

St. Lawrence Formation

Franconia Formation

sandstones and shaly sandstones
of the Galesville, Eau Claire, and Mt.
Simon formations

approximate level
of the
Mississippi River

Precambrian
rocks

Hinckley and Fond
du Lac formations

(crystalline igneous
and metamorphic)

rocks found only in the
subsurface

OLDEST ROCKS

The Rocks of Southeastern Minnesota, including Stockton Hill (modified from Austin, 1969)

Backwater of the Mississippi River near Wabasha.

19 Barn Bluff

Red Wing

COUNTY: **Goodhue**
NEAREST TOWN: **Red Wing**
OWNERSHIP: **City of Red Wing**
USGS TOPOGRAPHIC MAPS: **Red Wing, 7½´, 1974**

Barn Bluff rises abruptly some 300 feet above downtown Red Wing. It is composed of early Paleozoic rocks, displaced by a large fault. Its isolated character and oblong shape suggest its origin, several thousand years ago, as an island in the much-enlarged, postglacial Mississippi River. From its crest may be seen the present Mississippi River, other abandoned islands and stream channels, the Cannon River, Prairie Island, and Lake Pepin.

U.S. Highway 61 cuts along the southern flank of Barn Bluff immediately east of the interstate bridge at Red Wing. Follow the Barn Bluff signs posted along U.S. 61 to East Fifth Street. Follow this street eastward until it passes under the highway. Park beyond the underpass on either side of the road. A trail leads uphill past the reservoir on the west side of the road. There are interpretive signs along this trail and numerous vantage points. Once on top, the entire "mountain" is readily traversed. To view the large road cut at Barn Bluff's base, walk from the parking lot westward for one-half mile along U.S. 61.

Several hundred million years of history are compressed into the rock of Barn Bluff. The Cambrian sandstone, siltstone, and shale at its base grade slightly over halfway to the top into Ordovician sandstone and dolomite. These flat-lying sediments record the advance, retreat, environment, and life of the early Paleozoic seas. The dolomites indicate deep quiet water, the sandstones

shallow turbulent water. The greenish Franconia sandstone indicates an oxygen-deficient environment. The siltstones contain occasional trilobites, primitive marine arthropods.

The top 65 feet of Barn Bluff are covered by assorted glacial materials— sand, gravel, drift, and loess, wind-deposited silt. The break between the rock and "dirt" represents a hiatus of approximately 450 million years, a time during which Minnesota was subjected to erosion.

Another interesting feature of Barn Bluff is a fault, a dip-slip fault with an approximately 150-foot displacement (see Site #13). During the late Paleozoic the rocks of Barn Bluff split, shifted, and dropped. The plane of this fault is seen on the bluff where U.S. Highway 61 crosses U.S. Highway 53. The buff St. Lawrence siltstone on the northwest side of the fault contrasts markedly with the greenish Franconia sandstone on the southeast. Because of this faulting, the rock layers of Barn Bluff are 150 feet lower than those of neighboring Sorin's Bluff.

Sorin's Bluff and several other bluffs to the southeast were, like Barn Bluff, islands in the postglacial Mississippi. Stream channels separated these islands. Both the islands and channels are readily seen from the top of Barn Bluff. U.S. Highway 61 follows one of these channels from Red Wing to Lake City. As the water subsided to present levels, the islands were left as massive bluffs on an otherwise level plain.

The present Mississippi River and Lake Pepin are also seen from the top of Barn Bluff. At and above Red Wing the Mississippi is confused by numerous channels, islands, bars, and marshes. This maze results from the Mississippi depositing its sediment as it slows down on entering the broad expanse of Lake Pepin. The delta of Wisconsin's Chippewa River, formed where that river enters the Mississippi, partially dammed the Mississippi and caused this lake—a lake which is 50 feet deep, three miles wide, and 22 miles long.

Barn Bluff, with its sequence of Paleozoic rock, its fossils, its capping of loess and glacial drift, its eroded character, and its outstanding view of the Mississippi River, is an excellent introductory site for all of Southeastern Minnesota.

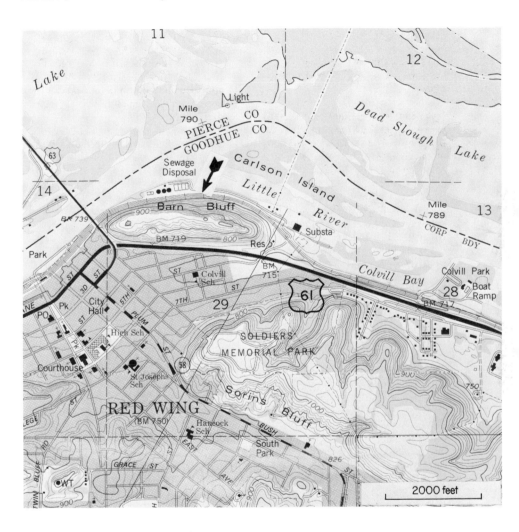

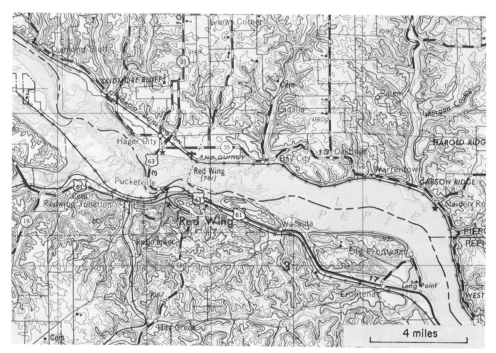

Barn Bluff, Red Wing, and a portion of the Mississippi River, including Lake Pepin, from the USGS St. Paul 1:250,000, 1953 map.

Barn Bluff, Red Wing.

Mississippi River

Buena Vista Park
Alma, Wisconsin

COUNTY: **Buffalo**
NEAREST TOWN: **Alma, Wisconsin**
OWNERSHIP: **City of Alma**
USGS TOPOGRAPHIC MAP: **Alma, 7½ ', 1974**

The Mississippi, with all its major tributaries, is North America's largest and longest river system. It is the fifth largest and the third longest river system in the world. It drains all or part of 31 states and two Canadian provinces. Its discharge is the eighth greatest in the world. The Mississippi River is one of the world's busiest commercial waterways and is the unruly neighbor of some of North America's richest farmland. The Mississippi winds among rounded glacial hills, cuts through high rock bluffs, and meanders across low marshy plains; it is diked, dammed, and monitored. The Mississippi has made a unique contribution to the history and literature of the United States. The river is a sight to be seen and savored.

A truly outstanding vantage point for the Misssissippi River is found at Buena Vista Park on the high bluff above Alma, Wisconsin. Alma is located on Wisconsin Highway 35, eight miles southeast of Wabasha, Minnesota. Follow the Buena Vista Park sign and County Road E eastward and up the hill at the south end of Alma. Continue on County Road E for 1.2 miles, then turn left, again following park signs, and proceed 1.3 miles to the park. From the bluff's edge, approximately 500 feet above the Mississippi, is a spectacular view of this mighty river and its broad valley.

The Mississippi begins in north central Minnesota as a small, shallow, clear-water stream. Five hundred sixty-eight miles (George Carlson, 1982, oral communication) later it leaves the state as a broad, rolling, dark-water river. During this passage, it has changed from a small, wild, forest-bordered wading stream to a broad, busy, highly controlled commercial waterway. Free, wild, and clear at its origin, it leaves the state confined by locks and dams and polluted by sewage, industrial waste, pesticides, and herbicides. Yet this river, monitored and controlled, exploited and revered, continues to make its way proudly and relentlessly across the heart of North America to the Gulf of Mexico. Year in and year out, season after season, it carries away the topsoil from the Central Lowlands and the Great Plains and deposits it on the Gulf Coast, advancing its delta six miles seaward every century. The river cuts new channels and fills old channels. In places the river flows unfettered through scattered young lakes. In other places it is confined within large, old bedrock valleys.

At Alma the river flows through such a bedrock valley—a valley almost six miles across and 600 feet deep, a valley developed in preglacial, glacial, and immediately postglacial times, a valley whose bedrock floor is 100 to 200 feet below its present alluvial floor. The valley began to develop sometime after the retreat of early Paleozoic seas from Southeastern Minnesota and was probably well established by glacial times, when glacial meltwaters coursed through this valley, greatly enlarging the river and its valley.

Since glacial times the river has rapidly diminished in size; it no longer fills the valley and scours its bedrock floor. The river instead has deposited clays, silts, sands, and gravels on its bed and along its margin. The river now occupies only a small portion of its huge valley, wandering back and forth across the valley floor. The Mississippi River valley has become a confusion of channels, backwaters, lakes, deltas, dunes, and islands. The water itself

20

runs freely in some places, but in most places it has become ponded by a series of dams—both man-made and natural, locks and dams for navigation and power, tributary-deposited deltas. Between the city of Minneapolis and the Iowa border there are eight locks and dams. There are two major deltas. The deltas, of Wisconsin's Chippewa and LaCrosse rivers, have produced Lakes Pepin and Onalaska.

From Buena Vista Park, high on a bluff of Ordovician dolomite on the east side of the Mississippi's bedrock valley, may be seen most of these valley and river features. The Mississippi spreads out above Alma, ponded by Lock and Dam No. 4. Below Alma the Mississippi meanders through a maze of islands, levees, and bars. The main channel of the Mississippi swings against the east side of the valley here, against the bluff at Alma, and leaves a large area of sand and silt, known as the Weaver Bottoms, on its western side.

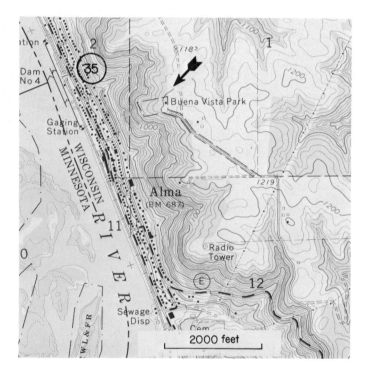

The Mississippi River and Alma, Wisconsin, from Buena Vista Park.

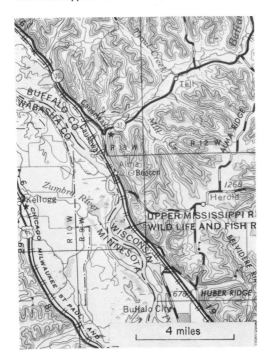

The Mississippi River and its tributaries near Alma, Wisconsin, from the USGS Eau Claire 1:250,000, 1953 (limited revision 1964) map.

21 Stockton Hill Sedimentary Sequence

Winona County

COUNTY: **Winona**
NEAREST TOWN: **Stockton**
OWNERSHIP: **Public roadway**
USGS TOPOGRAPHIC MAPS: **Rollingstone, 7½', 1972; Winona West, 7½', 1972**

One of Southeastern Minnesota's most complete sedimentary rock sequence is found in the road cuts of Stockton Hill. Over 400 feet of early Paleozoic rock are exposed along four winding scenic miles of U.S. Highway 14. These are the framework rocks for much of Southeastern Minnesota—the rocks which make up its hills and valleys, bluffs and slopes—rocks which are exposed here, but are usually covered by soil and vegetation. Gray dolomite (calcium-magnesium carbonate) and yellow sandstone dominate the sequence. Green siltstone and buff shale are also present. Calcite crystals and trilobite fossils are abundant in several of the layers. These rocks are similar to those at Barn Bluff (Site #19), but are more accessible and represent a greater segment of geologic time.

Stockton Hill is located between Stockton and Winona. U.S. Highway 14 climbs over this hill, producing scattered road cuts throughout the entire distance. The best way to appreciate this hill, its rocks and vistas, is to drive slowly from Winona to Stockton and back again. Drive very carefully; this is a busy highway with a great deal of truck traffic and several intersecting roads. The mileages given for the location of particular rock units begin at the small stream in Stockton and end four miles away at the Winona city limits sign near St. Mary's College.

Three Cambrian formations, rock layers, and two Ordovician formations are exposed at Stockton Hill. The Cambrian rocks are named the Franconia Formation, the St. Lawrence Formation, and the Jordan Sandstone. They are the oldest rocks. The Ordovician rocks are younger and lie on top of the Cambrian rocks. They are named the Oneota Dolomite and the Shakopee Formation. All of these rocks are flat lying and are the deposits of shallow continental seas.

The oldest and hence lowest rocks belong to the Franconia Formation. These shaly, greenish sandstones are seen along the north side of the road near the base of Stockton Hill, one-half mile from the stream at Stockton. The Franconia Formation is also seen on the opposite side of the hill at mile 3.7. The rock's green color comes from the mineral glauconite, a mineral common only in early Paleozoic rocks. This mineral may have been formed through the digestive action of marine worms. Overlying the Franconia Formation are the buff, fossil-bearing siltstones of the St. Lawrence Formation. They are seen 0.8 mile from the Stockton stream. Between these two road cuts and behind a barn and feedlot is a fresh exposure of both the Franconia and the St. Lawrence formations. This latter exposure is on private land. Note that the rocks of both these formations occur in thin layers, layers less than several inches thick. This is great contrast to the overlying sandstone and dolomite, whose layers are often many feet thick.

Midway up the hill, at mile 1.0, opposite milepost 252, is a large, very striking road cut of orange and yellow sandstone. This is the Jordan Sandstone. The soft white sand has been stained by iron and cemented by calcite. The degree of iron staining causes the yellow, orange, and brown color variations. The amount of calcite cement, hence the degree of weathering, causes the irregular layers and nodules. The Jordan Sandstone is found throughout much of East Central and Southeastern Minnesota. It is an excellent aquifer, or water-bearing layer. Most of the deep wells in the Twin Cities and other southern Minnesota towns derive their water from this formation.

Two hundred feet of thick-bedded, drab gray Oneota Dolomite overlie the Jordan Sandstone. This rock is conpicuous in road cuts toward the crest of Stockton Hill. Especially noteworthy are those on both sides of the road at mile 1.7 and again on the north side of the road at mile 2.8. Cavities, often filled with large calcite crystals, are seen in the upper portion of this formation. The Oneota Dolomite is used in concrete manufacture and is quarried on the north side of Stockton Hill at the intersection of Winona County Road 118. This is the resistant rock which caps the Mississippi River bluffs from Red Wing southward into Iowa.

The top 20 feet of Stockton Hill consists of soil, residual rock material, and irregular chunks of reddish sandstone. This is a highly weathered portion of the Shakopee Formation. It is seen best at mile 1.9, very near the crest of Stockton Hill.

Rocks younger than the Shakopee Formation were deposited in this vicinity but have since been removed through long periods of erosion. These younger rocks, however, may be seen further to the west. Many of them are exposed at Golden Hill (Site #22) in Rochester.

Rocks older than those exposed at Stockton Hill are encountered in deep wells at Winona. These wells cut through approximately 700 feet of younger Cambrian sediments—the Ironton Sandstone, Galesville Sandstone, Eau Claire Formation, and Mt. Simon Sandstone—before penetrating Precambrian granite at approximately 100 feet above sea level, 500 feet below the level of the Mississippi River (Thiel, 1944, pp. 470–71).

All of these rocks, except the granite, testify to the great length of time, several hundred million years or more, Southeastern Minnesota lay under early Paleozoic seas. Together they present an impressive record of a significant portion of geologic history.

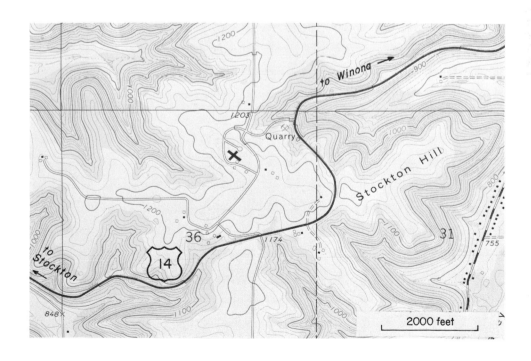

Road cuts at Stockton Hill. The rock in the foreground is the Jordan Sandstone; that in the background is the Oneota Dolomite.

The location of Stockton Hill from the USGS Eau Claire 1:250,000, 1953 (limited revision 1964) map.

Golden Hill
Sedimentary Sequence

Rochester

COUNTY: **Olmsted**
NEAREST TOWN: **Rochester**
OWNERSHIP: **Public roadway**
USGS TOPOGRAPHIC MAP: **Simpson, 7½',**
1974

Four major rock units are exposed at Golden Hill: the Glenwood Formation, the Platteville Formation, the Decorah Formation, and the Galena Formation. Their total exposed thickness is approximately 100 feet. The shales and limestones which dominate this sequence record the changing environmental conditions of a shallow Ordovician sea. Shales changed to limestones and back again; the sea became less and then again more sediment laden. Organisms changed accordingly. The various rock units weather differently, recede and slump or resist and project, and occupy different portions in the nearby landscape.

Golden Hill is located in Rochester along U.S. Highway 52, immediately south of the Zumbro River. Approach this site from the north, and park far off the right-hand shoulder below a low road cut 0.4 mile from the river. Examine this first low cut into the Glenwood and Plattville formations. Walk approximately one-quarter mile uphill to a second, far larger and longer road cut. This road cut exposes the Decorah and Galena formations. Walk to the south end of this 60-foot-high, one-half-mile-long exposure, examining the rocks along the way. Return along the east side of the highway. The total walk up and back is less than 1.5 miles.

Poorly exposed in the ditch at the very bottom of the first road cut is 1.5 feet of hard yellow sandstone, the very top

portion of the thin, shaly Glenwood Formation. This formation overlies a distinctive white rock, the St. Peter Sandstone (Site #54), which is entirely buried here but appears in outcrop one mile to the east in a cliff along the west side of U.S. Highway 63, behind the Country Kitchen. The St. Peter Sandstone in turn overlies the Shakopee Formation, a highly weathered dolomite seen at the top of Stockton Hill (Site #21).

The Shakopee dolomite was deposited in a quiet Ordovician sea. The sea retreated and an interval of erosion followed. Later in the Ordovician the sea again moved northward into Minnesota. Sands deposited along its margins, on its beaches, and in its shallows, wind winnowed and wave washed, became the clean St. Peter Sandstone. As the water deepened, muds carried seaward by streams and currents fell on the sea floor. They became the Glenwood Shale (Glenwood Formation).

As the water continued to deepen and quiet, limy materials were deposited: calcium carbonate from the warm seawater and the shells of numerous marine animals. The Platteville Formation, a 22-foot-thick limestone making up the bulk of this lower road cut, records this change. Within the gray-to-tan rock are many fossils, the remains of animals which inhabited this warm marine environment. Watch for, but do not collect, the numerous small shells found on the flat surfaces between the limestone beds.

Also within the Platteville Formation is a thin layer of soft white rock called bentonite. The bentonite, an altered volcanic ash, occurs approximately six feet below the top of the first road cut. This ash, from volcanoes somewhere in the southeastern United States, fell into the Platteville sea, settled on the sea floor, smothered the marine life, and marked a particular instant in geologic time. This ash can be traced throughout Southeastern Minnesota and into Wisconsin, Iowa, and Illinois. It serves,

22

therefore, as an extraordinary time reference—a correlative device often sought but rarely found within the rock record.

Slowly, more clay material moved into this quiet environment, life forms changed, and shale deposition again took place. The Decorah Formation records this change. It is the soft, gray-green, fossil-filled material (see Site #23) which falls away in the lower half of the upper, larger road cut. This shale weathers easily, slumps readily, and forms the gentle midslopes of the nearby hills. This formation is 47 feet thick at Golden Hill. If one foot of shale is laid down in 10,000 years, then 470,000 years of deposition are represented here. However, such figures grossly simplify matters: depositional rates are never precisely known and never uniform over time.

Once again the sea quieted and perhaps deepened. Carbonate clays, products of warm and quiet water deposition, replaced silicate clays, clastic sediments carried seaward by streams and rivers. Limestone replaced the shale. The upper 35 feet of Golden Hill consists of this younger limestone, the prominent Galena Formation. This resistant, gray-to-yellow, thick-bedded limestone overhangs the Decorah shale and caps the nearby hills. Its characteristic fossil is the circular "sunflower coral," *Receptaculites*, a mysterious organism, perhaps a type of green alga.

The Galena Formation completes the Ordovician sequence of marine shales and limestones found at Golden Hill. Younger Paleozoic rocks may only be seen farther southward in Minnesota, in the karst and cave country of Fillmore County (Sites #25 and #26).

Galena Limestone overlying the Decorah shale at Golden Hill, Rochester.

23 Ordovician Fossils

Goodhue County

COUNTY: **Goodhue**
NEAREST TOWN: **Goodhue**
OWNERSHIP: **Public roadway**
USGS TOPOGRAPHIC MAP: **White Rock, 7½',
1968**

Fossils may be found in practically any road cut or quarry in Southeastern Minnesota. However, some places and rock units are more productive than others. The Decorah Formation is a fossil display case par excellence. This is a soft, gray-green shale with several buff-colored limestone beds. Myriads of marine animals, from small mosslike bryozoans to large chambered cephalopods, are found throughout the formation.

An easily examined portion of the Decorah Formation is located in central Goodhue County. Begin at the intersection of Minnesota Highway 58 and Goodhue County Road 9 in the town of Goodhue. Follow Goodhue County Road 9 west for seven miles to its intersection with Goodhue County Road 8. This intersection is 3.8 miles east of U.S. Highway 52, eight miles south of Cannon Falls. The greenish Decorah Formation, overlying the buff Platteville Formation, is exposed on the west side of County Road 8, less than one-half mile north of Goodhue County Road 9.

Park far off to one side of the road, walk along the exposure, and find a likely place to sit down: small fossils are not seen from car windows or even from normal eye level. Fossils occur in both the abundant shale and the less abundant limestone layers of the Decorah Formation. Fossils may be collected here, as each rain renews the supply. The rain washes the fossils from the enclosing rock material and leaves them lying on the surface. Please, however, keep only those fossils which will be truly treasured. Leave the rest for others.

The rocks of the Decorah Formation were laid down in a warm, shallow Ordovician sea. Some 500 million years ago, this sea extended from the Gulf of Mexico northward into central Minnesota. Living on the quiet, well-lit sea floor were innumerable primitive marine organisms—corals, sponges, crinoids (stalked echinoderms), trilobites (primitive marine crustaceans), brachiopods ("lamp shells"), and molluscs (snails, cephalopods, and clams). All of these animals left their remains, now petrified and encased in the rocks. Other animals, as well as plants, undoubtedly lived here. These, however, were not preserved, through lack of hard body parts or the vagaries of chance.

The most common fossils are bryozoans. These are tiny colonial animals, very similar in external appearance to corals but possessing far more complex body systems. Their fossils look like small, flattened, branching sticks, dome-shaped gum drops, or thin, perforated crusts. Bryozoans live in modern seas and freshwater lakes. One of the few conspicuous freshwater bryozoans forms large, four- to six-inch, gelatinous masses. These are occasionally seen floating in the quiet, clean but weedy waters of Minnesota lakes.

Another common group of fossils are the brachiopods. These are marine shelled organisms, far more common in the past than they are today. As opposed to clams, brachiopods are bilaterally symmetrical organisms. Brachiopods are like people: their back and front sides are very different, their left and right sides very much the same. One of the more common brachiopods found in the Decorah Formation has a flattened, fanlike shell. Another has a small, ridged, nutlike shell.

Clams whose top and bottom shells look the same, but whose right and left sides are distinctly different, belong to a group of animals called molluscs.

Molluscs include not only the pelecypods (clams), but also the gastropods (snails) and cephalopods ("head-footed" molluscs). Clam and snail fossils usually occur here as internal molds. No shell material remains, only a rock impression of their internal configuration. This is also true of the cephalopods—shelled, squidlike organisms, the terror of the Ordovician seas. The cephalopods are Minnesota's most spectacular fossil, attaining lengths well in excess of 20 feet. Specimens of this size are best looked for in new quarrying operations. Cephalopods of several inches long are a good find for this location.

A child's favorite fossil is usually the small, pointed "cheerio." These are "stem" segments of the crinoid, or "sea lily." Crinoids are like starfish turned upside down and attached to the sea floor by long, flexible stalks. The "arms" of this animal are seldom found, but the stem segments are fairly common.

Horn corals, small cornucopialike affairs, are also found in the Decorah Formation. These were solitary animals, unlike those of today. Modern corals are colonial: they lived attached to one another, often forming large tropical reefs.

The most treasured and unusual find is the trilobite. They were primitive arthropods distantly related to the modern horseshoe crab. They crawled on the sea floor, burrowed into it, and swam above it. They were highly versatile, often highly ornamented "bugs." They ranged in length from nearly microscopic to over two feet. Those found here are closer to the former end of the scale. The trilobites are extremely interesting little creatures with an involved geologic history. Found rolled, as they often are, trilobites make a wonderful addition to any pocket or fossil collection. A good complete specimen, however, should be shown to a knowledgeable paleontologist. Such specimens are unusual and may even represent a yet unnamed species.

Collecting fossils in the Decorah Formation is good, albeit not always clean, family fun. In wet weather, shales return to their former consistency— mud.

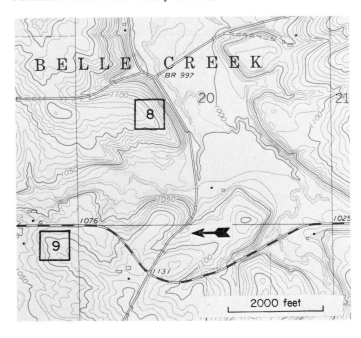

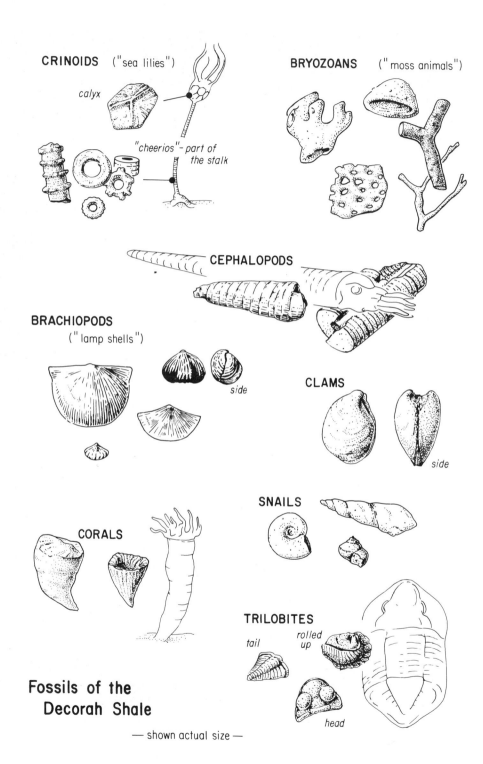

CRINOIDS ("sea lilies")

calyx

"cheerios" - part of the stalk

BRYOZOANS ("moss animals")

CEPHALOPODS

BRACHIOPODS ("lamp shells")

side

CLAMS

side

CORALS

SNAILS

TRILOBITES

tail

rolled up

head

Fossils of the Decorah Shale

— shown actual size —

Close-up of fossils in the Decorah Formation.

Road cut in the Decorah Formation. A small amount of limestone from the underlying Platte-ville Formation is seen in the lower right-hand corner of the photograph.

24 Driftless Area

Winona and Houston Counties

COUNTY: **Winona and Houston**
NEAREST TOWN: **Ridgeway**
OWNERSHIP: **Public roadway**
USGS TOPOGRAPHIC MAPS: **Houston, 15′, 1958; LaCrescent, 15′, 1956**

In extreme Southeastern Minnesota is a rugged, highly picturesque region of broad valleys separated by high, narrow, flat-topped ridges. This is a portion of the Driftless Area, a region encompassing approximately 15,000 square miles of Wisconsin, Minnesota, Iowa, and Illinois. In contrast to the surrounding lands, it apparently was never glaciated or was glaciated so early in the Pleistocene that little evidence of glaciation remains. Highlands to the northwest and northeast deflected most southward-flowing glacial ice. Thus, the landscape of this region is very old, highly dissected, and unlike that of the remainder of the Midwest. Thin rock spires and fragile sandstone peaks exist here. Bedrock is directly overlain, if at all, by a thin mantle of loess, lake or stream deposits, weathered rock material, and soil. Preglacial stream valleys, buried elsewhere, were simply enlarged in this region. In Minnesota this landscape is best seen in extreme southeastern Winona County and eastern Houston County (Schwartz and Thiel, 1954, p. 308).

A 30-mile round trip through the heart of this region begins and ends near Ridgeway in southern Winona County. Take the Witoka exit from Interstate 90. Proceed east and south on Winona County Road 11, which on entering Houston County becomes Houston County Road 9. Continue on this road to its intersection with Minnesota Highway 76 immediately north of Houston. Turn north on Minnesota Highway 76 and return to the point of origin.

Encountered along this route are flat cultivated uplands, steep wooded slopes, and broad open valleys. The total relief is approximately 650 feet. Level land occurs at about 1300 feet and below 800 feet. Between these two elevations the land is steep and rocky. The varying rock units which underlie this region erode differently and occupy different portions of the landscape. Underlying the uplands is approximately 200 feet of hard, resistant dolomite. Softer materials—shales, siltstones, and sandstones—crop out along the valley walls and underlie the valley floors.

The stream valleys encountered in this region are typical of the Driftless Area. Their dendritic, or branchlike, drainage pattern was developed on these flat-lying rocks over a long period of time. Well established before the Ice Age, these valleys were at times broadened, lengthened, and deepened by glacial meltwaters. With changes in the glacial regimen the broad valleys filled with fine alluvial material. Renewed downcutting of the streams then left remnants of these higher valley floors. These remnants are called stream terraces. They are seen along most of these valleys.

Begin the journey through the Driftless Area at the intersection of Minnesota Highway 76 and Winona County Road 11 at the interstate exit. Follow Winona County Road 11 eastward to Ridgeway. The gentle upland seen in this vicinity has developed on the resistant Oneota and Shakopee dolomites. Overlying the dolomite is only a thin layer of rock residuum, loess, and soil. A well in Ridgeway shows this unconsolidated material to be 20 feet thick (Thiel, 1944, p. 475).

From Ridgeway continue southeast on Winona County Road 11. At mile 6.7 the road makes a sharp right turn and begins a steep, winding descent off the upland and into the narrow, heavily wooded, rocky reaches of the Upper Looney Valley. The upland-forming dolomite is exposed in a large quarry at mile 7.1, on the left of the first major turn. Road cuts farther down the valley expose older, softer rock. The road levels off by mile 9. The drive is now along the broad floor of the Looney Valley.

The confluence of the Looney and Root valleys is seen at mile 12.3. Pull off the roadside at mile 13.6 and look eastward down the Root Valley. Note the broad, level expanse of the valley floor and its bordering terraces. The entire valley here is two miles across. This vantage point is on the edge of a particularly prominent, approximately 35-foot-high terrace. A farm just to the east of this vantage point is situated at the base of this terrace. To the west of here, St. Mary's Cemetery, a number of new homes, and a few older farms are also built on this landform of silt and fine sand.

From this vantage point drive westward, dropping over the terrace, continuing along its base, and following along the north side of the Root River. At mile 15.7 stop at the intersection of Houston County Road 9 and Minnesota Highway 76. Proceed straight ahead on Minnesota Highway 76, still following the base of the terrace. At mile 17.6 the terrace is pastured and begins to fall away eastward behind some large farm buildings. At mile 18.1 the highway climbs onto the terrace and enters the valley of Money Creek.

Stop part way up Money Creek at mile 19.4. The view to the east shows that very little of the upland remains in this vicinity. There are only a few isolated hills. The valley itself is flat bottomed and terraced similar to the Root Valley.

At mile 23 the road begins a distinct climb back to the uplands. Large road cuts expose soft Cambrian sandstones, silstones, and shales of the Franconia and St. Lawrence formations. There is a huge road cut in the yellow Jordan Sandstone and buff Oneota Dolomite at mile 27.

The trip ends back on the upland at mile 27.8, at the intersection of Minnesota Highway 76 and Winona County Road 11. Recommended further excursions through this Driftless Area are up the Wiscoy and Campbell valleys to the northwest and northeast of Money Creek. Both of these valleys are smaller, more confined, and more isolated than those seen on the principal route. Their gravel roads are not recommended during wet or icy conditions. However, the surrounding landscape is again very typical of Minnesota's Driftless Area.

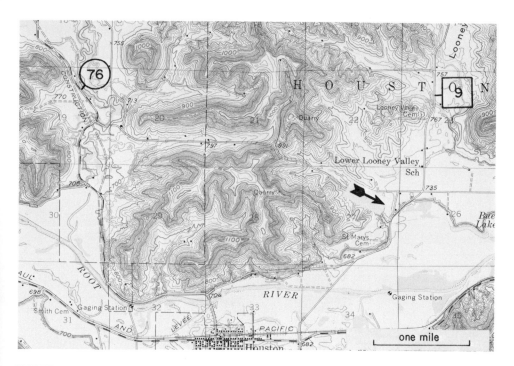

The Root River valley, bordering terraces, and dissected uplands, near Houston.

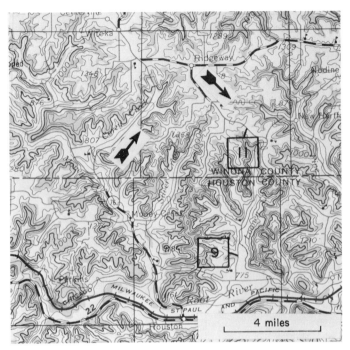

A portion of Minnesota's driftless area from the USGS LaCrosse
1:250,000, 1958 map. Interstate 94 is not shown in this map but crosses
the northern part of the map area, between Witoka and Ridgeway.

25 Karst Topography

Fillmore County

COUNTY: **Fillmore**
NEAREST TOWN: **Wykoff**
OWNERSHIP: **Public roadway**
USGS TOPOGRAPHIC MAPS: **Wykoff, 7½′,
1965; Fountain, 7½′, 1965**

A peculiar pitted landscape runs diagonally from northwest to southeast across Fillmore County. Neatly laid out corn and soybean fields are broken sporadically by small circular islands of trees. These islands are actually unplowed, steep-sided, rocky holes— sinks. These are the entrances to a strange underground maze. Beneath the orderly countryside is a dark labyrinth of irregular caverns and channels. Such a landscape of dissolved limestone is called karst.

An excellent and short drive through the sink-riddled country begins at Wykoff and ends 7.5 miles to the northeast at the village of Fountain. This route follows Minnesota Highway 80. Many sinks occur along both sides of the highway. They appear from the distance to be circular, isolated, or clumped patches of trees. In some places there are several of these per acre. They range in diameter from 30 to 150 feet across and in depth to 30 feet. Close inspection shows them to be steep, rocky, funnel shaped, and often full of old cars and tractors. Most are overgrown with bur oak, wild grape, stinging nettle, woodbine, and wild cherry. Most are dry. Some, however, are plugged and full of water. A small, water-filled sink occurs on the south side of the highway five miles from Wykoff. After heavy summer rains many of these sinks become mad, swirling vortices of dark water. In the course of several hours, or several days, this water usually sinks, slowly or rapidly, into the underground drainage system of Fillmore County.

Be sure to stop 3.7 miles east of Wykoff. North of the roadway is a whole array of sinks apparently arranged along a large underground channel. The land slopes gently toward these sinks from all directions, directing the runoff from heavy summer rains.

Karst topography develops through the dissolution of limestone. Limestone dissolves through the presence of weak carbonic acid. As rain falls, it incorporates atmospheric carbon dioxide and becomes slightly acidic. As this water seeps into the ground, it increases in acidity, picking up carbon dioxide from soil, air, and rotting plant tissues. The limestone dissolves rapidly on coming into contact with this weakly acidic water. The Galena Limestone of Fillmore County has been undergoing this dissolution process for perhaps 100 million years.

Karst topography thus develops in regions of moderate to high rainfall, where limestone occurs at or near the land surface. As the rainwater percolates into the fractures of the limestone, it dissolves the rock, leaving it pitted and cavernous. Over time the limestone becomes more cavernous, and big sections begin to collapse. This countryside, at first simply pockmarked as here in Fillmore County, becomes more and more irregular and treacherous, as in Jamaica's impassable cockpit country. Eventually most of the limestone is dissolved, and only steep pinnacles remain. This is called tower karst. Such a landscape occurs in South China. The strange dreamlike quality of paintings depicting this region are not the figments of some artist's inebriated imagination: they are only slight exaggerations of reality.

The karst of Southeastern Minnesota, which occurs in all the counties adjacent to the Mississippi River and as far west as Olmsted and Fillmore counties, reaches its greatest degree of development in Fillmore County. There are an estimated 5750 sinks in this county. One farmer counted 40 sinks in one 80-acre patch (Oberdorfer, 1981, p.

10B). This is significant karst development, yet it does not hold a candle to that of Jamaica or South China, and without an extreme change in Minnesota's climatic regime, probably never will.

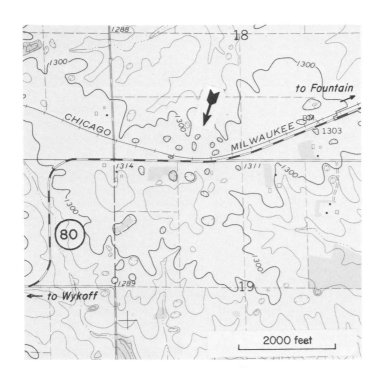

Sinks in a corn field near Wykoff.

26 Mystery Cave

Fillmore County

COUNTY: **Fillmore**
NEAREST TOWN: **Spring Valley**
OWNERSHIP: **Private**
USGS TOPOGRAPHIC MAPS: **Cherry Grove,
7½', 1965; Wykoff, 7½', 1965**

Mystery Cave is the longest cave in the
Upper Mississippi River valley. There
are more than 15 miles of known
passageways, two entrances, and
scheduled commercial tours. This interesting and wet limestone cave is
located in the valley of the South
Branch Root River, the waters of which
flow through the cave's lower passages.
The cave also has dripping water,
standing pools, and numerous,
multicolored flowstone deposites. It is
never entirely silent.

The cave is located approximately six
miles southeast of Spring Valley. Beginning in Spring Valley, watch for direction signs to Mystery Cave. Follow
U.S. Highway 63 south for 4.7 miles
from its intersection in Spring Valley
with Minnesota Highway 16. Turn east
on the gravel road opposite the Bloom-
field Town Hall. Follow this road east
for 3.5 miles, turn right beyond the
Lone Oak Cemetery, and continue
following the road for another 0.5 mile
until it crosses over the South Branch
Root River. Turn right immediately and
proceed 0.5 mile to a parking lot.
Follow a short path over a slight rise
and down across the footbridge back
over the river. On the west end of the
bridge is a picnic ground, campground,
and information building. Tickets for
the cave tour may be purchased here.
Entrance #1 is located just east of the
foot bridge. Entrance #2 is 1.5 miles to
the northeast of here; the cave guide
will direct you to it.
  Neal Davie is the present owner and
operator of Mystery Cave, which is

open seven days a week from Memorial
Day to Labor Day. Tours begin at
10:00 a.m. and finish at 4:00 p.m. The
admission is $4 for adults and $2 for
children. Children under six years are
free. The commercial section of the
cave is easy walking, relatively level,
well lighted, and safe. The cave
temperature is 47° throughout the year.
A sweater or light jacket is necessary.
For more information write or call:
Neal Davie, Route 2, Mystery Cave,
Spring Valley, Minnesota 55975.
Phone: (507) 937-3251.

Minnesota has more than 300 known
caves; however, only three of these are
commercial caves and open to the
public. Mystery Cave is the most
diverse of these commercial caves. It
has more than 12 miles of mapped
passageways, 1.5 miles of which are on
the two commercial routes. The tour
from Entrance #1 takes about an hour
and covers 0.5 mile. The tour from
Entrance #2 is about twice as long. The
portion of the cave seen near entrance
#1 has developed in the Dubuque For-
mation, approximately 34 feet of olive
gray limestone with interbedded shale.
The main passage here trends northeast,
is 10 to 20 feet wide, and six to 30 feet
high. There are short intersecting
passages. The portion of the cave seen
near Entrance #2 has developed in the
Galena Formation. This portion of the
cave has larger passages and more
cross-passages than seen near Entrance
#1. It also feels wilder. On both tours
will be seen a small lake and a variety
of cave deposits, including stalactites,
stalagmites, and flowstone. There are
numerous fossils of brachiopods,
cephalopods, trilobites, and graptolites.
There are few bats.
  Minnesota's two other commercial
caves are Niagara Cave and Stillwater
Caves. Niagara Cave, like Mystery
Cave, is a limestone cave. It is located
approximately 12 miles southeast of
Mystery Cave and approximately five
miles southwest of Harmony. This is a
deep, single-passage cave with a very

dramatic sinkhole entrance. It boasts a large underground waterfall. The second cave, Stillwater Caves, is a sandstone cave and is located at the south end of Main Street in Stillwater. This cave, consisting of a series of rooms, extends some 300 feet into the hillside. These rooms were once used for aging beer.

The majority of Minnesota's caves are in limestone and occur in the southeastern portion of the state, particularly in Fillmore and Olmsted counties. However, there are numerous sandstone caves, somewhat similar to Stillwater Caves, near Winona, Red Wing, and in the Twin Cities. These sandstone caves are smaller and generally better known than the limestone caves. They have often been enlarged and used, among other things, for mushroom production, boat storage, and cheese holding (Site #54).

Mystery Cave was formed through solution along joints in the Ordovician Galena, Maquoketa, and Dubuque formations. These formations are predominantly limestone, a rock which dissolves readily in the presence of the weak carbonic acid of normal rain and groundwater (see Site #25). Development of this cave system was probably initiated during the Cretaceous (Sloan and Weiss, *in* Schwartz, 1956, p. 100). The solution accelerated during the Pleistocene. The cave is still enlarging,

now not only through solution, but also through scour: small streams run through this cave. The cave's multicolored flowstone deposits formed in comparatively recent time, since perhaps the earliest glaciers (Ibid.). Flowstone deposition occurs when groundwater, saturated with calcium carbonate, evaporates within a rock cavity. The calcium carbonate precipitates in the form of flowstone.

Mystery Cave has 12 miles of mapped passageways, and over three more miles of known passages. New passages are being discovered and mapped each year. The portions of the cave seen near Entrance #1 and Entrance #2 were once believed to be separate caves and were known respectively as Mystery Cave and Minnesota Caverns. They are now known to belong the same large cave system. The walk and crawl and squeeze from Entrance #1 to Entrance #2 takes approximately 10 hours. This particular cave, as well as many of Minnesota's other limestone caves, still holds many secrets, surprises, and mysteries. And although Mystery Cave is not Carlsbad Caverns, an hour or two spent in its dark recesses may be rewarded by a more thorough understanding of all limestone caverns and a deep and growing sense of curiosity and adventure.

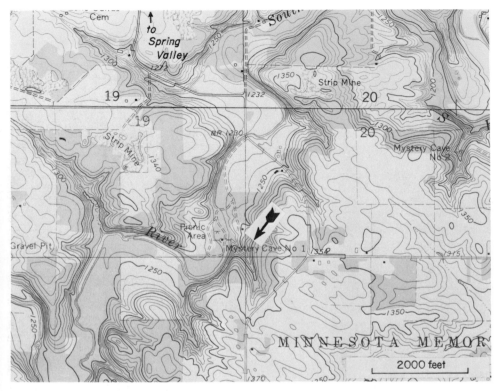

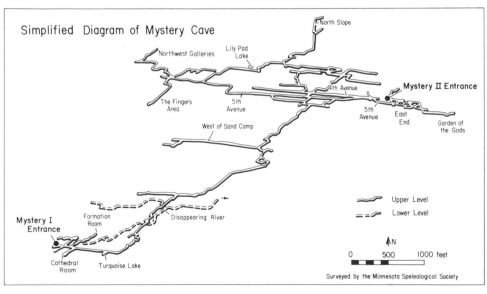

Simplified Diagram of Mystery Cave

North Slope

Northwest Galleries

Lily Pad Lake

Mystery II Entrance

4th Avenue

The Fingers Area

5th Avenue

5th Avenue

East End

Garden of the Gods

West of Sand Camp

Upper Level

Lower Level

Disappearing River

Mystery I Entrance

Formation Room

Cathedral Room

Turquoise Lake

N

0   500   1000 feet

Surveyed by the Minnesota Speleological Society

Entrance 1 to Mystery Cave, Spring Valley.

Minnesota River valley near Granite Falls, Southwestern Minnesota.

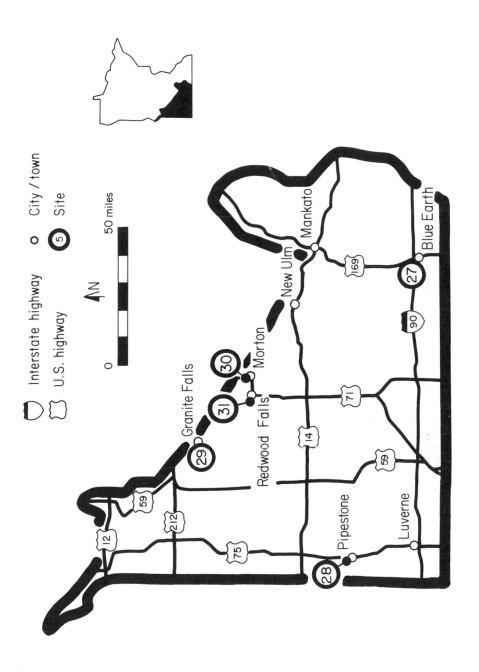

Interstate highway

U.S. highway

City / town

⑤ Site

N

0 ——————— 50 miles

12
59
212
75
28
29 Granite Falls
31
30 Morton
Redwood Falls
14
71
59
169
27 Blue Earth
90
New Ulm
Mankato
Pipestone
Luverne

III Southwestern Minnesota

Till Plain and Ground Moraine, the Minnesota River Valley and Archean Rocks

Most of Southwestern Minnesota is a level to mildly undulating plain, its bedrock skeleton obscured by a thick mantle of glacial drift. This region, once a sea of prairie grass, has now been broken by the plow to become a patchwork of cultivated fields, neat farmsteads, and narrow windbreaks. The deep fertile soils, developed over the past 12,000 years, have made this region the heart of Minnesota's corn belt. The rivers have well-established drainage patterns. Lakes occur only in a few broad upland depressions. However, bordering the gentle till plain is the high moraine-edged, rock-centered Coteau des Prairies and the sharp-edged, rock-bottomed Minnesota River valley. The coteau is underlain by glacial drift, Precambrian quartzite, and various Cretaceous sediments. Exposed in the Minnesota River valley are some of the world's oldest rocks, Archean granites and gneisses. Southwestern Minnesota ranges from an elevation of over 2100 feet on the crest of the Coteau des Prairies to less than 730 feet in the valley of the Minnesota River.

Southwestern Minnesota is bounded on the south by Iowa, on the west by South Dakota, and on the northeast by the Minnesota River valley. It is bounded on the east by the high, hilly, lake-strewn country of the Owatonna moraine complex, which runs southward from Jordan through New Prague, Waterville, Waseca, and Albert Lea.

The Blue Earth till plain is a region of gently rolling ground moraine. This ground moraine, consisting of a gray, shale-rich calcareous till, was deposited by the rapidly melting Des Moines lobe, the last glacier which advanced over Southwestern Minnesota. This glacier retreated from the area—that is, melted—approximately 12,000 years ago. After glacial retreat a spruce-fir boreal forest covered Southwestern Minnesota. Then as the climate warmed and dried, prairie invaded the region. Southwestern Minnesota's rich agricultural soils have developed under the luxuriant prairie grasses.

The Coteau des Prairies is a broad, flatiron-shaped regional highland occupying the southwestern corner of Southwestern Minnesota and the adjacent parts of South Dakota and Iowa. The highland is probably underlain by bedrock, but much of its topographic prominence is due to a thick—in places as much as 700-foot-thick—blanket of glacial drift. The edge of this highland is marked by moraines, often highly subdued, denoting the margins of the Des Moines lobe ice and other older ice sheets.

The Minnesota River valley, Southwestern Minnesota's most scenic feature, is a long, narrow window into the Precambrian. This broad valley extends in a straight course for 180 miles from its head at Browns Valley to the big bend at Mankato. There it turns northeastward, running for another 40 miles through the hilly morainic country of West Central Minnesota and on to its confluence with the Mississippi River in the Twin Cities of Minneapolis and St. Paul. The Minnesota River itself is a sluggish, winding stream, almost dwarfed by its broad, deep, glacial-meltwater-carved valley.

Rocks and geologic materials median in age between the recent glacial drift of the Blue Earth till plain and the ancient Precambrian gneisses of the Minnesota River valley are seen in several places in Southwestern Minnesota. The Sioux Quartzite, a late Precambrian sheet sandstone, crops out prominently on the Coteau des Prairies between Luverne and Pipestone. A thick layer of clay formed during the Cretaceous crops out in the vicinity of Redwood Falls. Buff Cretaceous sandstones containing fossils leaves occur near New Ulm, and Cretaceous shales containing abundant sharks' teeth occur at the head of Big Stone Lake. The Precambrian rocks, Cretaceous clays, glacial drift, and varying topographic features of Southwestern Minnesota tell a geologic story of extreme metamorphism, shallow seas, tropical climate, and glacial advance and retreat.

Blue Earth till plain from the air, late autumn, Southwestern Minnesota.

Blue Earth Till Plain

Guckeen, Faribault County

COUNTY: **Faribault**
NEAREST TOWN: **Guckeen**
OWNERSHIP: **Public roadway**
USGS TOPOGRAPHIC MAP: **Huntley, 7½',**
1967

Much of Southwestern Minnesota has a relatively level, slightly rolling landscape underlain by thick glacial drift, unsorted rock debris dropped by a melting glacier. Such a subdued landscape of glacial drift, or till, is known as a till plain. It is the result of rapid glacial melt over a broad area. This particular till plain, known as the Blue Earth till plain, is not outstanding in and of itself: there are other till plains throughout Minnesota and the Midwest. The geologic significance of this till plain lies in the fact that it is characteristic of other till plains. However, the economic significance of this till plain in particular and others in general almost cannot be overstated. The deep, rich prairie soils of this region, developed on the many feet of gently sloped glacial drift, have made this the heart of Minnesota's corn belt, in an area already called the bread basket of the world.

One of the most satisfactory places to view the gentle cultivated land of the Blue Earth till plain is on the overpass across Interstate 90, approximately six miles west of Blue Earth. Take the Guckeen-Huntley exit from Interstate 90 onto Faribault County Road 1. Turn off the roadway at the northwest corner of this intersection and look in all directions. Everywhere is the smooth, cultivated countryside of corn and soybean fields—scattered homestead and adjacent windbreaks, red barns, blue or gray silos, dark, easily managed soils.

This is a scene repeated over and over again throughout the till plains of the Midwest.

27

The Blue Earth till plain begins south of the Minnesota River and extends to the Iowa border. It runs westward from the hills of the Owatonna moraine complex near Waseca to the base of the Coteau des Prairies near Walnut Grove. This area was covered during Minnesota's most recent glaciation by the central part of the Des Moines lobe, a glacier which flowed into this region from Northwestern Minnesota. The ice coursed down the Red River and Minnesota River lowlands, spreading across Southwestern Minnesota and into Iowa as far south as Des Moines. The ice reached Des Moines approximately 14,000 years ago (Wright, *in* Sims and Morey, 1972, p. 540). During the next 2000 years the ice melted back out of Iowa and Southwestern Minnesota and into the Red River lowland. The rapidly melting glacier left behind at least 100 feet of limy, gray, shale-filled drift, which covered the bedrock, old drift, and preexisting topography. The resulting landscape is highly muted, with almost imperceptible hills and swales and a few broad, shallow lakes.

After glacial retreat the region was quickly covered by spruce forest. Later, as the climate warmed and dried, prairie grasses invaded the region. The growth and decay of the luxuriant prairie grasses have over the past 9000 or so years changed the structure, texture, organic content, and chemistry of the fresh glacial drift. Fertile, well-textured soils one foot or more in thickness have developed over the entire region. These are the soils which have made this land so agriculturally valuable.

The Blue Earth till plain often means monotony to the freeway driver, a livelihood to the farmer, a rapidly melting glacier to the geologist, and a breakfast to many.

Blue Earth till plain near Guckeen.

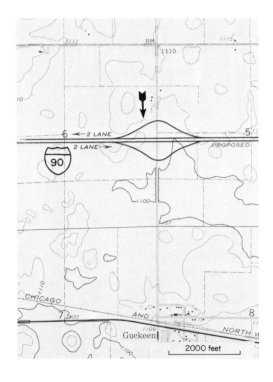

Coteau des Prairies and Sioux Quartzite

Pipestone National Monument

COUNTY: **Pipestone**
NEAREST TOWN: **Pipestone**
OWNERSHIP: **U.S. Government**
USGS TOPOGRAPHIC MAP: **Pipestone North, 7½', 1967**

The Coteau des Prairies, "highland of the prairies," occupies the extreme southwestern corner of Minnesota and adjacent parts of extreme eastern South Dakota and northeastern Iowa. It is underlain variously by glacial drift, Cretaceous sediments, and a hard, pinkish, late Precambrian sandstone known as the Sioux Quartzite. The coteau is important simply because it is a well-known physiographic feature. The Sioux Quartzite is important as one of several midwestern Precambrian sheet quartzites and is most well known for its thin layers of pipestone. Pipestone National Monument, located on the crest of the Coteau des Prairies, preserves a scenic ridge of Sioux Quartzite and nearby pipestone quarries. Included within the monument is an outstanding interpretive center and a network of hiking and nature trails. Along with the quartzite and pipestone, the monument has preserved many of the native prairie plants and the primal prairie scene.

Pipestone National Monument is located north of the city of Pipestone, 0.5 mile northwest of the intersection of U.S. Highway 75 and Minnesota Highway 23. From this intersection proceed north 0.3 mile on U.S. Highway 75. Turn west and follow the monument signs 0.5 mile to the monument entrance. Proceed to the visitors' center, park, and walk around the center examining its many exhibits. Hike along the footpaths to the quarries and ridges. Before leaving the monument, visit the Three Maidens, pieces of a huge glacial erratic located in the southeastern part of the park.

The Coteau des Prairies, a flat-topped highland, is bordered on the west by the James River lowland and on the northeast by the Minnesota River lowland. The wedge-shaped, north-pointing upland formed before glacial times as a high region between major river basins. During glacial times it served to split the southward moving ice sheets into the James River lobe on the west and the Des Moines lobe on the east. The coteau is most well known for its steep, almost 1000-foot-high, east-facing scarp, a portion of which may be seen in Redwood County between Tracy and Walnut Grove.

The Sioux Quartzite underlies portions of the Coteau des Prairies. It overlies middle and early Precambrian rocks and is overlain occasionally by various Cretaceous sediments and often many feet of glacial drift. The quartzite crops out in Nicollet, Rock, Pipestone, Cottonwood, Watonwan, and Brown counties. It may be seen at Pipestone National Monument, Blue Mounds State Park, and Jeffers. A 30-foot cliff of Sioux Quartzite runs northward from Luverne to the Rock County line.

The quartzite, usually pinkish in color but varying from nearly white to a deep reddish purple color, is a relatively thin rock layer of great areal extent. It is similar and presumably equivalent to the Baraboo and Waterloo quartzites of Wisconsin (Sims and Morey, *in* Sims and Morey, 1972, p. 10). It is believed to be between 1.4 and 1.5 billion years old (Ibid.) and appears to have formed in shallow water, possibly on the edge of a shallow sea. This rock, along with other midwestern quartzites, indicates that in late Precambrian times this portion of North America was relatively stable and quiet. It was not subject to the massive mountain building, lava extrusions, or faulting of earlier times.

By far the greatest bulk of the Sioux

Quartzite is a clean quartz sandstone, firmly cemented by silica which has been deposited by saturated groundwater and colored by varying amounts of iron oxide. However, its thin siltstone, or catlinite, layers have made it famous. Catlinite, named after the famous nineteenth century painter George Catlin, is also known as pipestone. This smooth, soft, red rock carves easily and hardens on exposure to air. North American Indians quarried this pipestone for approximately three centuries, using the rock for their ceremonial pipes and other objects. The quarries and displays at Pipestone National Monument tell this story.

Trail and Sioux Quartzite at Pipestone National Monument.

29 Minnesota River Valley

Granite Falls

COUNTY: Yellow Medicine
NEAREST TOWN: Granite Falls
OWNERSHIP: Public roadway
USGS TOPOGRAPHIC MAP: Granite Falls,
7½', 1965

The large Minnesota River valley, steep sided and often rock floored, cuts across all of central Minnesota, extending from Browns Valley on Minnesota's western border to Minneapolis on Minnesota's eastern border. In its western portion the valley cuts deeply into high, gentle till plains; to the east it cuts through rugged, hilly moraines. The valley contains a great diversity of geologic features—rock islands, rock and alluvial terraces, and elevated potholes. These features all tell the tale of Glacial River Warren, the large, powerful river which originated in Glacial Lake Agassiz (see the introduction to Region V) and cut this valley between 9000 and 12,000 years ago. Today this valley is occupied by the diminutive Minnesota River.

The best way to appreciate this huge valley and its unique scoured floor is to drive northward along Minnesota Highway 23 from two miles south of Granite Falls to Granite Falls. Begin at the intersection of Minnesota highways 23 and 274. Proceed the two miles north to Granite Falls. Within that distance the highway drops off the upland and onto the floor of the Minnesota River valley.

From the highway intersection, near milepost 101, look north into and across the Minnesota River valley, the huge channel of Glacial River Warren. A perspective on the valley size is gained by the Granite Falls power plant. At 0.3 mile a large side ravine enters the main valley east of the highway. At 0.6 mile the highway begins to drop off the

upland. Again look across the valley toward the power plant. Note the scoured, irregular, and hummocky ground. Look eastward down the length of the valley and note the steep valley sides and the flat, cultivated valley floor. The Minnesota River, dwarfed within this valley, cannot be seen from here but is immediately behind a line of trees and two cement-block silos. Continue on toward Granite Falls, noting the scoured valley floor. Granite Falls Memorial Park is immediately east of the intersection of Minnesota highways 23 and 67 in Granite Falls, and there the dark ridges and knobs of the valley floor may be explored on foot.

The Minnesota River valley, possibly established before glacial times, was the course of numerous meltwater streams. However, late in glacial times, as the last ice sheet retreated from western Minnesota, a huge lake formed in what is now the Red River valley. Waters of this lake, known as Glacial Lake Agassiz, flowed southeastward across central Minnesota. This outlet stream quickly became the huge, highly erosive river named Glacial River Warren. This river, emptying the waters of Glacial Lake Agassiz, cut through several hundred feet of glacial debris and into the underlying Precambrian and early Paleozoic bedrock. It cut the huge Minnesota River valley, which is now as much as five miles wide and 250 feet deep. This river cut terraces along the valley wall and scoured the valley floor. The peculiar landscape within the valley at Granite Falls is the result of differential stream erosion. The rock ridges, knobs, and channels have resulted from the river scour and the structure of the exposed Precambrian rock.

Such a scoured landscape is highly unusual, and it is found only where large rivers or floods have streamlined and washed bare the landscape. The Columbia Plateau in eastern Washington and adjacent parts of Oregon and Idaho, in a region known as the Channelled Scablands, has a similar landscape. The land surface there, as here, is a maze of channels, bars, and islands. The landscape here formed on the floor of a mighty river; there as the result of a short-lived, catastrophic flood.

Once Glacial Lake Agassiz had found an outlet to the north, Glacial River Warren was beheaded and diminished rapidly to become the far smaller and quieter Minnesota River. The Minnesota River, unable to carry away all of the debris brought into its valley by its tributary streams, has become a silt-laden, meandering stream interrupted by large, shallow lakes. The Minnesota River valley has become partially filled by stream debris and segmented by alluvial fans.

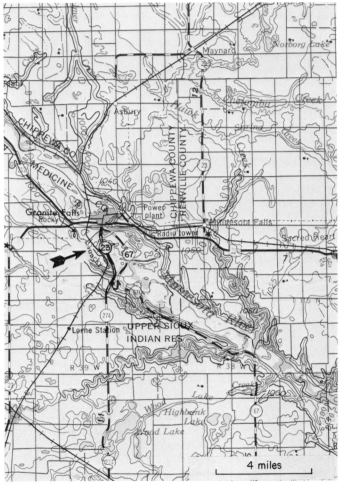

The Minnesota River valley near Granite Falls, from the USGS New Ulm 1:250,000, 1953 (limited revision 1967) map.

Irregular scoured landscape in Minnesota River valley at Granite Falls.

Granite erratic in the Minnesota River valley near Granite Falls. This erratic has been flattened through the erosive action of Glacial River Warren.

Morton Gneiss

Morton

COUNTY: **Renville**
NEAREST TOWN: **Morton**
OWNERSHIP: **Various—private individuals and corporations, City of Morton, State of Minnesota**
USGS TOPOGRAPHIC MAP: **Morton, 15', 1952**

One of the world's oldest rocks, the Morton Gneiss, is exposed on a rock knob within the Minnesota River valley near Morton. This ancient and complex metamorphic rock, dated at 3.5 billion years, is equal to or exceeded in age only by similar gneisses in the Godthaab district of West Greenland. Consequently, a great deal of geologic investigation has been expended on this rock—its age relationships, mineralogy, and geologic history. This site is hardly dull—it is one of the most interesting in Minnesota. The site is accessible and scenic, a wonderful place to explore with children and a camera. Beware, however, of the water-filled quarry and the high pile of quarried rock. Besides rock, there is a variety of unusual plants. Please examine, photograph, and enjoy these plants, but do not disturb them.

Note also that this outcrop is owned by various individuals and organizations—be extremely sensitive to their ownership. Be careful, be quiet—take only pictures, leave nothing. Please stay on the rocks immediately behind the Morton school, which are State of Minnesota property, or near the quarry which is soon to be city of Morton property (John Seehausen, Sept. 1982, oral communication).

This outcrop of Morton Gneiss is on the northwest corner of Morton, on the northeast side of the intersection of U.S. Highway 71 and Minnesota Highway 19. Before visiting the outcrop, drive north to the cemetery, owned by the city of Morton, along U.S. Highway 71 approximately one mile from its intersection with Minnesota Highway 19. The cemetery overlooks Morton and the outcrop of Morton Gneiss. Note the relationship of this rock knob to the Minnesota River valley. The knob was once an island in Glacial River Warren (see Site #29). Note also the handsome headstones made from the red and gray Morton Gneiss.

Visit the rock knob, the outcrop of Morton Gneiss. Return to the intersection of U.S. Highway 71 and Minnesota Highway 19. Turn east on Minnesota Highway 19 and proceed approximately one-quarter mile. Turn north on the first street, Fifth Avenue, past the schoolhouse. Park along Fifth Avenue and walk quietly through the school grounds. Hike westward onto the rocks. To gain access to the old quarry, continue northward past the school approximately two blocks, then turn west on a dirt road passing by a wire fence. Follow the dirt road to the quarry.

The gray, red, and black swirled rocks of this site are known as gneiss (pronounced "nice"), and as the sign says upon entering Morton, don't take them for granite ("granted"). Gneiss is a banded, coarse-grained rock. The Morton Gneiss, with a composition similar to granite, has an abundance of quartz, feldspar, and the dark minerals biotite and amphibolite. Metamorphism, the exposure to great heat and pressure, has segregated these minerals into multicolored bands and swirls. The Morton Gneiss may be seen throughout the Sacred Heart–Morton area as well as in the Granite Falls–Montevideo area.

The Morton Gneiss has a complicated history of extreme metamorphism and deformation which has masked the rock's original character and obscured its age. However, it is believed that the rock was originally of igneous origin (Sims and Morey, *in* Sims and Morey, 1972, p. 8). Some time after this igneous rock had cooled and hardened, it was partially remelted, folded, and metamorphosed (Grant, Himmelberg, and Goldich, 1972, p. 16). Later, dark-colored dikes cut through this changed rock.

There have been extensive studies attempting to date these rocks and to unravel their history. It appears that the rocks were formed approximately 3.6 billion years ago and that they underwent major deformation and partial melting approximately 2.6 billion years ago. This partial melting accounts for the common swirling of this rock. Minor deformation of this rock took place until about 1.6 billion years ago (Ibid.). Since then the rock has remained remarkably stable.

Relative ages of rock can be determined by noting the field relationship one rock bears to another. For example, in flat-lying sedimentary rocks, those rocks higher in the rock sequence are younger than those rocks lower in the sequence (see Site #21). In igneous rocks, younger rocks cut across older rocks (see Site #17).

Absolute rock ages, however, must be determined by other means: erosional rates, depositional rates, radioactive decay rates. The Morton Gneiss may be dated radiometrically. Certain elements within particular minerals undergo radioactive decay over long periods of time. The rate of decay is known, and the amount of decay may be measured—the rock's age can then be determined. Such minerals as mica, hornblende, feldspar, and zircon can all be used in this dating process.

Through this process of radiometric dating it has been determined that the Morton Gneiss is far older than rocks elsewhere in Minnesota and also in most parts of the world. The much more commonly seen and still ancient Precambrian rocks of Northeastern Minnesota are more than one billion years younger than this gneiss. Rocks of

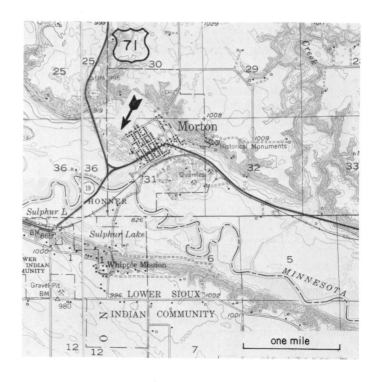

Southeastern Minnesota, of early Paleozoic age, are more than two billion years younger than this gneiss. The age of Minnesota's Cretaceous rocks and Pleistocene glacial deposits dwindle into complete insignificance beside the Morton Gneiss.

Small potholes scoured into the Morton Gneiss by Glacial River Warren.

Outcrop of Morton Gneiss, Morton.

31 Cretaceous Clay

Alexander Ramsey Park, Redwood Falls

COUNTY: **Redwood**
NEAREST TOWN: **Redwood Falls**
OWNERSHIP: **City of Redwood Falls**
USGS TOPOGRAPHIC MAP: **Redwood Falls, 15', 1952**

High banks of whitish clay occur along the Redwood River near Redwood Falls. This clay, the weathering product of the ancient Morton Gneiss (Site #30), could only have formed under a tropical climate: the minerals within the gneiss decompose into clay only under warm, moist environmental conditions. The clay has thus been studied in an attempt to discover when such a climate may have occurred. It has also been studied in an attempt to more thoroughly document the sequence of mineral decomposition.

Alexander Ramsey Park is located on the northwest side of Redwood Falls along the Redwood River and Ramsey Creek. Exit northward from Minnesota Highway 19 immediately west of its bridge over the Redwood River. Drive approximately six blocks to the park's entrance. Follow the winding park down the valley past Ramsey Creek and over the Redwood River. Just beyond the Redwood River, turn left onto the gravel road leading toward the picnic area and campground. Stop near the rock picnic shelter and walk down to the river. Near the river is a bronze plaque explaining the local geology. Across the river are the high, light-colored cliffs of clay.

Careful study of this Redwood Falls clay has led geologists to believe that a humid tropical or semitropical climate was present in Minnesota during the Cretaceous, some 100 million years ago. At that time the world's climate as a whole was far more uniform than today, perhaps due to the existence of broad continental seas. After this time, as the Cretaceous seas retreated off the continents, the world's climatic zones became more differentiated and pronounced. Minnesota slowly developed its mid-latitude, mid-continental climate. No longer could exposed granitic rocks decompose into clay in its cold, relatively dry atmosphere.

Clays similar to those seen at Redwood Falls are forming today in Hong Kong. The granites of Hong Kong, like the gneisses of Redwood Falls, are broken down into their constituent minerals, which in turn decompose into clay. The feldspars and micas incorporate water into their molecular structure and change to clay. The abundant quartz, however, highly resistant to this type of decomposition, remains within the clay as small, angular pieces of sand.

This decomposition, or weathering, is the response of minerals, once formed in equilibrium with conditions deep within the earth's crust, to new conditions upon the earth's crust. At formation the minerals were subject to high temperature and pressure; now they are subject to much lower temperatures and pressures. They are also in contact with air, water, and various organisms. On exposure, different minerals behave differently. Minerals formed at higher temperatures and pressures decompose faster than those formed at lower temperatures and pressures. That is, certain minerals are more stable on the earth's surface than others.

S. S. Goldich, a Minnesota geologist, has traced the sequence of mineral alteration at Redwood Falls. He has traced the change of the hard gneiss into a soft clay. Geologists elsewhere have studied the same type of occurrence and in each case have found that certain minerals decompose faster than others. In particular, the dark-colored minerals—hornblende and biotite—decompose faster than the light-colored minerals—orthoclase feldspar and muscovite. Quartz is always highly resistant to decomposition.

Thus the clays at Redwood Falls, not particularly striking to look at nor appealing to hold, tell a long, involved geologic story. They tell the story of a great change in Minnesota's climate over the past 100 million years. They tell a second story of involved, yet systematic, mineral decomposition.

Banks of Cretaceous clay along the Redwood River, Alexander Ramsey Park, Redwood Falls.

Typical rolling landscape of West Central Minnesota, near Lonsdale.

Lake Itasca and high wooded shores, West Central Minnesota.

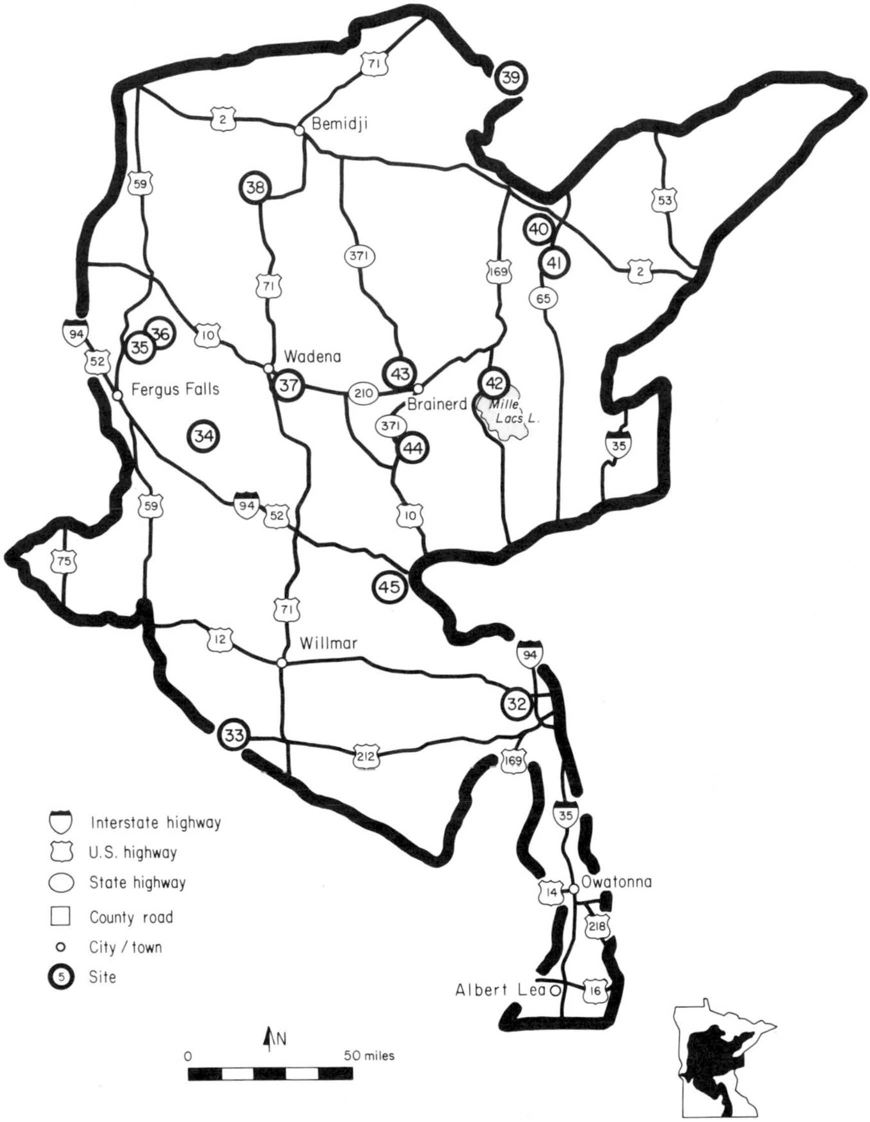

71
39
2
Bemidji
59
38
53
40
371
169
41
2
71
65
94
36
10
35
Wadena
52
43
42
Fergus Falls
37
210
Brainerd
Mille Lacs L.
371
34
44
35
94
59
52
10
75
45
71
12
Willmar
94
32
33
212
169
35
Interstate highway
U.S. highway
State highway
County road
City / town
5
Site
14
Owatonna
218
Albert Lea
16
N
0
50 miles

IV West Central Minnesota

Lakes and Moraines

West Central Minnesota is a region of lakes and moraines. Its young landscape is the direct result of Minnesota's most recent glaciation. The whole array of glacial landforms characterizes West Central Minnesota—end moraines and ground moraines, outwash plains and till plains, eskers, and drumlins and kames. Wherever there are depressions, there are lakes and wetlands. And there are depressions, lakes, and wetlands everywhere—big and small, round and oblong, shallow and deep, weedy and clear, sandy and mucky, cattail fringed and tamarack fringed, muskeg filled and spruce filled. This is prime recreational land, land for hunters, fisherman, and hikers. Much of this region is also prime agricultural land, land for dairy cattle, corn, alfalfa, and soybeans.

This region encompasses much of the central portion of Minnesota, from Bemidji to Albert Lea, from Fergus Falls to Sandstone. It is bounded on the northeast by outcrops of ancient Precambrian rock. It is bounded on the southeast by the more dissected land surfaces of older glaciations and the Paleozoic rock exposures of Southeastern Minnesota. It is bounded on the southwest by the Minnesota River valley and on the northwest by the young, lacustrine lake plain of Glacial Lake Agassiz.

End moraines—high, hilly, lake strewn, and often wooded—are formed as glacial debris piles up at the terminus of melting ice. One of the largest and most rugged of these, the Alexandria moraine, extends in a broad arc from Park Rapids to Detroit Lakes, Alexandria, Litchfield, and Buffalo. Another major terminal, or end, moraine runs through New Prague, Owatonna, and Albert Lea. Ground moraines form level to gently rolling till plains and develop when glaciers melt rapidly over broad areas. Such till plains are seen north of the Minnesota River valley and east of the Agassiz lake plain—near Winthrop, Olivia, and Callaway. Outwash plains—sandy, often level, and sometimes pockmarked with lakes—form at glacial margins where glacial meltwaters pour off the ice, spread out in all directions, and deposit their loads of silt, sand, and gravel. Outwash plains are seen near Brainerd, Grand Rapids, and Park Rapids. Eskers, high sinuous ridges of sorted sand and gravel, the pathways of subglacial streams, are seen scattered throughout West Central Minnesota, at Itasca and Scenic state parks, near Pine City and Sandstone, near St. Rosa, Faribault, and Albert Lea. Drumlins, elongate hills of unsorted glacial debris, occur in swarms near the towns of Wadena, Automba, and Toimi. Kames, high conical hills of stratified sands and gravels, are abundant near Lakes Lida, Itasca, Sandwick, and Minnetonka.

These hills, plains, and lake basins are all the result of the Wisconsin glaciation. This glaciation, the most recent of four Pleistocene glaciations, began approximately 40,000 years ago and ended approximately 10,000 years ago. Glaciers approached Minnesota from the northeast, north, and northwest, moving down the Superior, Rainy, Red Lake, and Red River lowlands and spreading out across the state. The moving ice incorporated rocks from the underlying terrane. As the ice melted, these rocks were dropped far from their place of origin. These rocks, known as glacial erratics, help define the paths of glacial movement.

Erratics are common, but exposed bedrock is uncommon in West Central Minnesota. In most places tens or even hundreds of feet of glacial debris cover the bedrock, which ranges in age from Precambrian to Cretaceous.

West Central Minnesota is thus defined by its unmistakable overprint of young glacial features. It is characterized by an abundance of lakes and streams, irregular hills, and occasional plains. The land is both wooded and open, pastured and cultivated. It is both recreational land and agricultural land. This amazing landscape diversity is the scenic result of the Wisconsin glaciation.

32 Lake Minnetonka

Hennepin County

COUNTY: **Hennepin**
NEAREST TOWN: **Excelsior**
OWNERSHIP: **Various**
USGS TOPOGRAPHIC MAPS: **Lake Minnetonka, 15', 1958; Minneapolis, 15', 1954**

Lake Minnetonka epitomizes the lakes and moraines of West Central Minnesota. It has formed through the partial drowning of knobs and kettles—the irregular hills and holes of a high end morainal belt. Its numerous bays, points, islands, and bars reflect the lake's glacial inheritance. They also reflect the action of more recent waves, currents, and ice. Lake Minnetonka is Minnesota's tenth largest lake and lies alongside the western edge of Minnesota's largest metropolitan area. The lake offers fine fishing, swimming, and boating. Winding roads pass along its scenic residential shores.

Perhaps the most enjoyable way to see the lake is by small open boat on a calm summer's day. Spend all the daylight hours on the lake, with fishingpole, swimsuit, picnic lunch, and family.

A second, perhaps more practical and easier way to see Minnetonka is to circle the lower lake by automobile. It is approximately an hour's drive from Excelsior through Navarre, Wayzata, Deephaven, and back to Excelsior. Follow Hennepin County Road 19, Hennepin County Road 15, Minnesota Highway 101, and Hennepin County Road 5.

Begin at Solberg Point in Excelsior. This is a city park situated at the north end of town on Lake Minnetonka. Drive southward through town to Hennepin County Road 19. Follow that road across the narrows to Navarre. At Navarre turn east on Hennepin County Road 15. Proceed alongside Lafayette Bay, across the Crystal Bay Bridge, and along Smith and Browns bays to Wayzata. From Wayzata turn back southward to Excelsior, following first Minnesota Highway 101 and then Hennepin County Road 5.

All manner of glacial features may be seen along this route. Several large conical hills known as kames are seen north of Browns Bay and alongside St. Albans Bay. Numerous bays, lakes, and swamps, known as ice-block depressions and formed through the melting of buried chunks of glacial ice, are also visible. Crystal Bay, rounded in outline and more than 70 feet deep, is an excellent example of such an ice-block depression. The numerous small and large rocks seen on this route are glacial erratics. These rocks have been glacially transported from elsewhere: all the bedrock in this area is buried beneath more than 150 feet of glacial drift.

The glacial geology of the Lake Minnetonka area is complex. The lake sits at the convergence of two major lowlands, the Lake Superior on the northeast and the Red River on the northwest. Glacial ice came down both lowlands and converged near Minnetonka, leaving a belt of high morainal hills. The ice from the Superior basin brought a red, sandy drift which may be seen in gravel pits northeast of Wayzata. Shortly afterwards ice from the Red River lowland spread into the region and brought with it a clayey, shale-filled, yellowish drift. Bluffs of this clay till may be seen along Big Island. This is the till most often exposed during highway and house construction.

Along the shores of Lake Minnetonka may also be seen many recent lake features—stony bars, sand beaches, and ice ramparts. These features have been built up through currents, waves, and ice. A long stone point known as Hardscrabble Point protrudes into Cook's Bay. A broad sand beach is found on the east side of Robinson Bay. A small but typical ice rampart is seen along the shore of Smith Bay.

The irregular, wooded, and sandy shores of Lake Minnetonka have made it a prime residential and recreational spot since the middle 1800s. In this century heavy usage put tremendous strains on the lake, and for some years its quality deteriorated rapidly. A major cleanup campaign was begun in the early 1960s. Marine toilets were banned, domestic and municipal sewage was prohibited from running into the lake, and agricultural runoff was carefully controlled. This campaign has been reasonably successful. The lake is now the site of the Gray Freshwater Biological Institute and is being carefully studied in an attempt to understand the dynamics of this particular freshwater system. The water quality is being carefully monitored. This unique lake is being preserved for future generations.

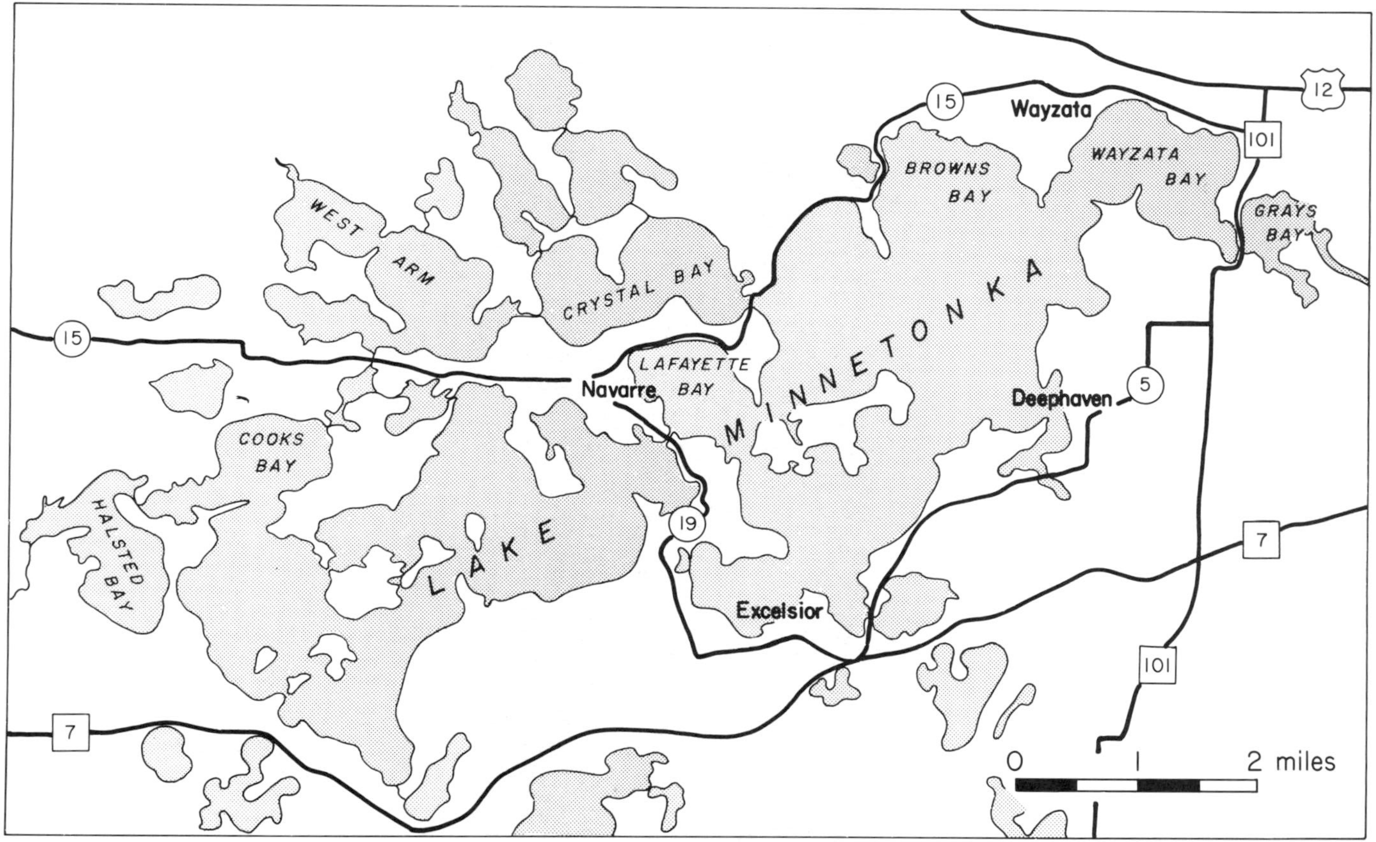

Lake Minnetonka, a large irregular lake in an end moraine.

HALSTED BAY

COOKS BAY

WEST ARM

CRYSTAL BAY

LAKE

Navarre

LAFAYETTE BAY

Excelsior

MINNETONKA

BROWNS BAY

Deephaven

WAYZATA BAY

Wayzata

GRAYS BAY

7

15

19

5

15

101

12

101

7

0   1   2 miles

Lake Minnetonka.

33 Glacial Tills

Renville County

COUNTY: **Renville**
NEAREST TOWN: **Sacred Heart**
OWNERSHIP: **Public roadway**
USGS TOPOGRAPHIC MAP: **Lone Tree Lake,
7', 1965**

Several different glaciers advanced over Minnesota during the Pleistocene. As the glaciers melted they left behind tills of varying color, texture, and composition. Two distinct glacial tills are exposed along Renville County Road 10 in extreme southwestern Renville County. They are separated by a conspicuous stoneline and a thick layer of outwash sand and gravel. These tills, glacially deposited mixtures of clays, silts, sands, gravels, and boulders, differ in color, texture, and composition. They are the deposits of two separate ice sheets that advanced over this area during the Wisconsin glaciation. The intervening stoneline may represent a time of erosion; the outwash represents a time of stream deposition. This exposure is unique in that the two tills and the stoneline are conspicuous. It is also unique in that the stoneline and upper till are separated by outwash, an occurrence not previously noted within this vicinity. Please respect this unusual and scientifically valuable exposure. In particular, take care not to disturb the boulders.

This exposure is along Renville County Road 10, near the confluence of Hawk Creek and the Minnesota River. The exposure is approximately 10 miles southeast of Granite Falls and four miles southwest of Sacred Heart. From Sacred Heart follow U.S. Highway 212 west 2.4 miles to Renville County Road 10. Turn south on Renville County Road 10 and follow it 4.3 miles. Park far off the road and examine the exposure along the west side of the road.

North of the Minnesota River in Chippewa and Renville counties are two distinctive glacial tills. These are commonly separated by a stoneline. The lower till, depending on lighting conditions and moisture content, is gray in color and a sandy loam (an equal mixture of silt, sand, and clay) in texture. The stones within this till, some to boulder size, consist primarily of granite, gneiss, basalt, diorite, and limestone. The upper till is a buff color and a clay loam. It has some large stones of granite, gneiss, and limestone. It includes many small pieces of gray shale. The intervening stoneline consists of rounded stones and boulders of granite, gneiss, and limestone. There is some diorite and basalt. The boulders at this site are rounded and range up to several feet in diameter. The outwash, found here but absent elsewhere, consists of stratified sands and gravel—with granite, gneiss, limestone, and gray shale.

During the Wisconsin glaciation the ice moved into Minnesota from the northeast, north, and northwest. As the glaciers moved over these regions they incorporated fragments of the underlying bedrock. When the ice melted, these rocks were deposited far from their origins. Since the rocks of northeastern, north central, northwestern Minnesota, and adjacent parts of Canada are distinctive, it is not difficult to trace their source. Glaciers moving from northeastern Minnesota through the Superior lowland carried rocks of gabbro, basalt, red felsite, and red sandstone. This lobe of ice, called the Superior lobe, left a reddish sandy-to-stony drift. Glaciers moving from north central Minnesota through the Rainy Lake region—the Rainy lobe—left a drift of variable color (generally a light brown) and variable composition, with undiagnositic granitic and gneissic rocks. Further west the Wadena lobe brought gray and buff, sandy and limy till from an area in Manitoba. Glaciers moving from northwestern Minnesota down the Red River lowland carried Paleozoic limestone and dolomite and light greenish gray Cretaceous shale. This glacier, called the Des Moines lobe, left a limy and silty till containing fragments of shale, limestone, and granite. This till is generally buff in color.

The lower grayish till in western Renville County was deposited by the Wadena lobe ice. This lower till is called the Granite Falls Till. The upper buff-colored till was deposited by glaciers moving from the Red River lowland, the Des Moines lobe ice. This upper till is called the New Ulm Till. Material from the bottom of the Granite Falls Till has been dated at around 36,000 years old (Matsch, Tipton, Steece, Rutford, and Parham, 1972, p. 13). Material at the top of the New Ulm Till has been dated around 11,000 years old (Ibid., p. 14). Both of these tills have served as parent material for the rich agricultural soils of western Minnesota.

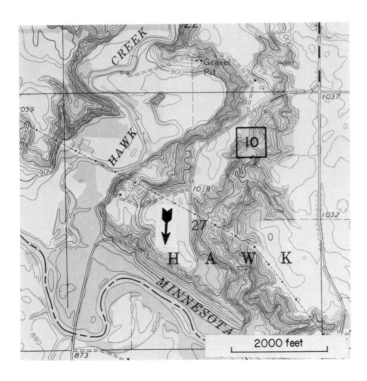

Renville County road cut exposing Granite Falls till overlain by New Ulm till. Separating the tills is a stoneline and layer of outwash sand and gravel.

Outwash sand and gravel overlain by New Ulm till.

Alexandria Moraine I

Inspiration Peak
State Wayside

COUNTY: **Otter Tail**
NEAREST TOWN: **Urbank**
OWNERSHIP: **State of Minnesota**
USGS TOPOGRAPHIC MAP: **Inspiration Peak,
7½', 1969**

Inspiration Peak is a vantage point for
the Leaf Hills, a particularly rugged
portion of the Alexandria moraine, the
large terminal moraine which extends in
a broad arc through West Central
Minnesota from Park Rapids to Buffalo.
Hilly, lake-strewn, and partially wooded
countryside is seen in all directions
from the top of Inspiration Peak—a
landscape typical of this west central
region. This site is a Minnesota state
wayside and an excellent and safe place
for children, picnics, and hikes.

Inspiration Peak is located in
southeastern Otter Tail County approximately 22 miles northwest of Alexandria and 12 miles northeast of Ashby.
Ashby is located 2.5 miles north of Interstate 94 on Grant County Road 10.
From Ashby follow Minnesota Highway
78 northeastward for five miles to the
intersection of Otter Tail County Road
38. Turn east on 38 and continue 6.5
miles to Inspiration Peak.

On the west side of Inspiration Peak
is a parking area, picnic ground, and
information sign. A paved circular trail
begins here and leads to the top. The
trail has an elevation gain of approximately 190 feet and a length of approximately 0.5 mile. A leisurely walk
around the loop will take 20 to 30
minutes. Climb up the gentler north
side and return down the steeper south
side.

Inspiration Peak, high and conical, is a
particular type of glacial hill known as

a kame (see Site #35). Other prominent
kames lie approximately one mile
southeast of Inspiration Peak. The
peak's open crest, 1750 feet above sea
level and 400 feet above nearby Spitzer
Lake, provides a panorama of rolling
hills and numerous shining lakes. This
morainal landscape has some of the
greatest local relief and landform diversity in Minnesota.

Inspiration Peak, like some other
parts of the Alexandria moraine, is on
Minnesota's prairie-forest boundary.
The lower, moister, more protected portion of the peak is hardwood forest.
The upper, drier, more exposed portion
is open prairie. These lower slopes are
primarily oak woods. Bur and northern
pin oak predominate. Within the oak
woods are occasional paper birch, large-
toothed aspen, ironwood, dogwood, and
nannyberry. It appears that this hill was
once grazed: poison ivy and prickly ash
are common. The open prairie toward
the top of the hill supports blazing star,
leadplant, purple bush clover, sage,
asters, and goldenrod. In April the soft
pasqueflowers appear in last year's
dried grass.

Inspiration Peak provides an overview
of the morainal landscape of West Central Minnesota. It provides an introduction to the Alexandria moraine. This
glacial landscape and moraine may be
thoroughly explored at Maplewood State
Park, Site #35.

34

2000 feet

View of the rolling, lake-strewn country of the Alexandria moraine, looking northeast from Inspiration Peak.

35 Alexandria Moraine II

Maplewood State Park

COUNTY: **Otter Tail**
NEAREST TOWN: **Pelican Rapids**
OWNERSHIP: **State of Minnesota**
USGS TOPOGRAPHIC MAPS: **Lake Lida, 7½',
1973; Heilberger Lake, 7½', 1973.**

Like Inspiration Peak (Site #34),
Maplewood State Park is located within
a very rolling, scenic portion of the
Alexandria moraine. In contrast to Inspiration Peak, however, which is a
vantage point, this is an approximately
9000-acre park in which the hills and
marshes and lakes may be thoroughly
explored not only by eye but also by
foot. Perhaps the most renowned feature
of this park is its large, numerous, and
highly characteristic kames, conical hills
of stratified sands and gravels. Also
notable are the park's approximately 50
lakes of varying sizes and shapes. This
park boasts numerous hiking trails,
three campgrounds, two picnic grounds,
a swimming beach, and two boat-
launching sites. Like Inspiration Peak,
Maplewood State Park is located on
Minnesota's prairie-forest boundary.
Maplewood's diversity of glacial
features, vegetation, and recreational
facilities make this park particularly appealing for the entire family.

Maplewood State Park is located seven
miles east of Pelican Rapids along
Minnesota Highway 108. The park entrance is approximately 1.5 miles east
of Lake Lida. Turn south into the park
and proceed to the information center.
Entrance fees must be paid there, and a
park information brochure and map are
available. For further information write:
Park Manager, Maplewood State Park,
Route 3, Box 281, Pelican Rapids, Minnesota 56572. Phone: (218) 863-8383.

Maplewood State Park lies wholly
within the Alexandria moraine—the
great belt of lake-dotted end moraine
which extends in an arc 10 to 20 miles
wide and nearly 200 miles long through
West Central Minnesota. The glacial
drift, up to several hundred feet thick,
consists of yellowish material from the
Des Moines lobe overlying grayish
material from the Wadena lobe. Northward this moraine gives way to
moraines of the Itasca and Bemidji
areas. Southward, near the Twin Cities,
it merges with the St. Croix moraine.

This portion of the Alexandria
moraine was last covered by active ice
approximately 12,000 years ago (H. E.
Wright, Jr., 1982, oral communication).
Several hundred years later Glacial
Lake Agassiz (see introduction to
Region V) had formed, and stagnant ice
may have persisted in the moraine.
Imagine standing then on the top of a
newly formed kame within this park.
Glacial Lake Agassiz would be seen
shining and endless, beginning less than
20 miles to the west. Dirty, rock-strewn
glacial ice would be broken and piled to
the northeast. Raw and very irregular
land would be seen to the south.
Perhaps far to the south would be seen
a dark spruce forest.

The most noteworthy features of this
park, its kames, are seen as concentric
circles on the topographic map. On the
ground they are recognized as high,
conical hills. Kames form when glacial
meltwaters deposit their loads of sand
and gravel within a depression of the
ice. When the ice melts this depression
filling is left as a hill. Kames also form
along the front of a glacier where
meltwaters have poured off the glacier's
surface and into an angle within the ice
front. Again a hill of sorted sands and
gravels is formed.

There are four particularly classic and
visible kames within the park. Three
are in the northwest portion of the park.
One kame is between the two park
roads leading to the picnic grounds;
another is approximately one-quarter
mile north of the northern picnic
ground. The highly symmetric, completely wooded island in the south arm

of Lake Lida is the third kame. This kame is attached to shore near the swimming beach by a rocky bar, undoubtedly formed through a combination of current, wave, and ice action. The fourth particularly notable kame is the large island in Twenty-One Lake in the southeast corner of the park. Throughout the park are many other kames.

The park is also renowned for its great number of lakes. These lakes range from highly regular to highly irregular in outline, from shallow to deep. Their surface elevations range from 1314 feet to 1423 feet. They have formed in ice-block depressions (see Site #44) or simply in low, water-filled, irregular portions of the landscape. Such a variety and number of lakes is common within the morainal belts of West Central Minnesota.

The vegetation in Maplewood State Park is also worthy of examination. The park lies near the sharp western edge of the Alexandria moraine, on Minnesota's prairie-forest boundary. Within this park are many of the typical prairie plants— big and little bluestem, Indian grass, prairie clover, and blazing star. The deciduous forest is characterized by sugar maple, American basswood, paper birch, elm, oak, ironwood, and ash. Bur oak is present in open savannahs— an interesting vegetational combination of grass and trees.

The prairies and forests, hills and lakes of Maplewood State Park are being carefully observed and managed. Enjoy them and learn from them.

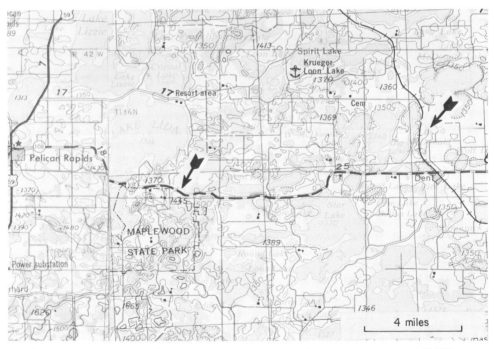

The Alexandria moraine in the vicinity of Maplewood State Park, from the USGS Fargo 1:250,000, 1953 (revised 1975) map and the USGS Brainerd 1:250,000, 1953 (revised 1975) map. Both Maplewood State Park and Big McDonald Lake (Site #36) are shown here.

Kame in Maplewood State Park.

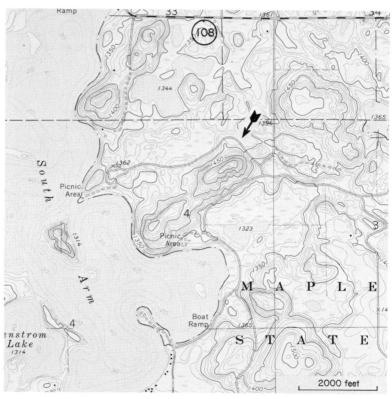

A portion of Maplewood State Park, showing its numerous and large kames.

Shore Features

Big McDonald Lake, Otter Tail County

COUNTY: **Otter Tail**
NEAREST TOWN: **Dent**
OWNERSHIP: **Public roadway and lake access**
USGS TOPOGRAPHIC MAPS: **Star Lake, 7½', 1973; Dent, 7½', 1973**

Big McDonald Lake is an outstanding example of a large ice-block lake which over time has become segregated into many smaller lakes. Water and ice have redistributed the sand of the lake's shores and bottoms. Waves, currents, and ice have built shoals, bars, points, and ramparts—shore features evident everywhere along this lake.

Big McDonald Lake is located between Dent and Vergas, approximately 18 miles south of Detroit Lakes. Begin in Dent, located on Minnesota Highway 108, and circle counterclockwise around Big McDonald Lake. Follow Otter Tail County Road 35 to Otter Tail County Road 121. Turn south on County Road 121 and follow it until it intersects with Minnesota Highway 108. Turn east on Highway 108 and return to Dent.

A quick circuit of this lake takes less than one-half hour. However, take several hours. Drive slowly and stop at the public access on the northwest side of the lake; drive past Archie Lake and examine the ice ramparts there. Everywhere note low, sandy shores, the bordering sand ridges, and the numerous small lakes, including Hoffman and Alice, which are separated from Big McDonald Lake by only a narrow spit of land.

Minnesota has well over 10,000 lakes, lakes which have formed in a multitude of ways—through ice scour of bedrock basins, the melting of glacial ice blocks, stream erosion and deposition, beaver damming, and moraine damming among others. Big McDonald appears to have formed through the melting of one or more buried blocks of glacial ice, the most common type of lake found within the state.

Once lake basins have formed through whatever means, water and ice continuously modify the original configuration. They constantly break down and redistribute the lakeshore materials. This is particularly evident with lakes like Big McDonald, which have formed in sand. Waves break down the shores, making their material available for current transport. Lake currents move the material along the shore and out into the lake. The currents then drop the material and build up bars, points, and shoals of all kinds. Ice, on the other hand, simply pushes the shore material into low parallel ridges called ice ramparts (Site #42). Ice often pushes underwater shoals, points, and bars above lake level.

Big McDonald Lake has been greatly modified by waves, currents, and ice. All along and within this lake are shoals, points, bars, and ice ramparts. Water and ice have rounded the outline of a large, irregular lake. Small bays have everywhere been isolated from the main lake by the construction of natural barriers across their mouths. Currents have build sandbars across these bays, and ice has raised these sandbars above the water. These bays have then become other lakes. Brown Lake has been cut off from West McDonald Lake. Alice Lake has been cut off from Hoffman Lake. Hoffman Lake has in turn been cut off from West McDonald Lake, and West McDonald Lake has been cut off from Big McDonald Lake. Archie, Mud, Reames, Walde, and Berger lakes have all been cut off from Big McDonald Lake. Big McDonald Lake itself has been split in half. In the 9000 years since ice retreat, waves, currents, and ice have vastly modified the basin of this lake—filled in the shallow areas, extended the points, raised them above lake level, and cut off the bays.

Many other lakes in Minnesota show the kinds of lakeshore features which are so clearly seen at Big McDonald Lake. Others worth noting in this particular area are: Marian Lake, 1.5 miles east of Dent, which is being cut in half by a bar extending from its south side; Loon Lake, approximately two miles north of Big McDonald Lake, which is overrun with bars, points, and ice ramparts; and Rusch, Paul, and Kerbs lakes, immediately northeast of Big McDonald Lake, which were once bays of Little McDonald Lake and are separated from that lake by bars and ice ramparts. Lake Johanna, in extreme southeastern Polk County, has a bar cutting east-west across it. Lake LeHomme Dieu, near Alexandria, is being divided east-west by Government Point and north-south by Tolena Point. That lake has probably already been separated by bars and ramparts from Lakes Carlos, Geneva, and Victoria. Ice ramparts also are particularly evident along Woman Lake near Longville, Leech Lake near Walker, North Long Lake near Brainerd (see Site #43), and Mille Lacs Lake near Wealthwood (Site #42).

Ice rampart on the shore of Big McDonald Lake.

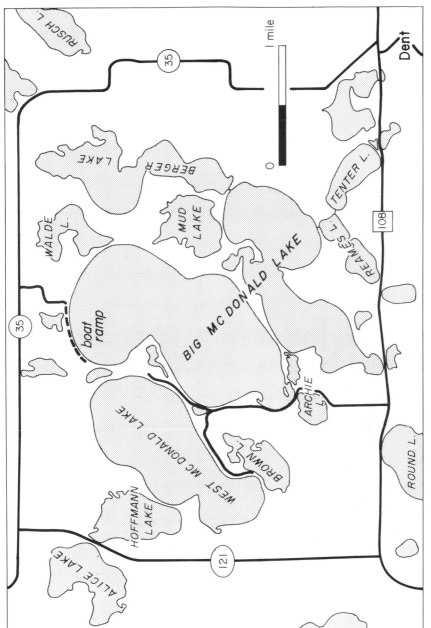

Big McDonald and nearby lakes, showing the rounded outline resulting from melted ice and the action of lake currents and lake ice.

37 Wadena Drumlins

Todd County

COUNTY: **Todd**
NEAREST TOWN: **Aldrich**
OWNERSHIP: **Public roadway**
USGS TOPOGRAPHIC MAP: **Aldrich South, 7½', 1966; Bertha, 7½', 1969**

Drumlins cover a large area of West Central Minnesota: nearly all of Wadena County, approximately half of Todd County, and adjoining parts of Cass, Hubbard, and Otter Tail counties. They are elongate hills composed of glacial drift and are usually found in groups known as drumlin fields or drumlin swarms. Their orientation indicates the direction of glacial movement, but their exact origin is under debate. Drumlin fields are found not only within Minnesota but also throughout the glaciated portions of North America and the world.

Perhaps the best place to see the Wadena drumlins is along Todd County Road 11 and Minnesota Highway 210 between Aldrich and Hewitt. The county road is nearly level and parallels the drumlins; the highway is a "roller coaster" road cutting across the drumlins. The distance between Aldrich and Hewitt is approximately 10 miles. Proceed south from Aldrich on Todd County Road 11 for 3.5 miles. Turn west onto Minnesota Highway 210 and drive 6.8 miles to Hewitt.

A particularly prominent drumlin runs through sections 10 and 15, Bartlett Township, approximately 2.5 miles south of Aldrich, 0.5 mile west of the county road. Balsamlund Church sits on its crest. Other drumlins exist everywhere along this route. The drumlins, however, are difficult to see, since the various land uses—field, pasture, and forest—cut across rather than along the drumlins. The drumlins here generally range between 30 and 60 feet high and one-half to three miles long. They are most readily seen and understood by studying the topographic map.

The Wadena drumlin field consists of approximately 1200 drumlins (Hogberg and Matsch, *in* Phinney, ed., [1967], p. 14), and records the earliest ice advance of the Wisconsin glaciation. The drumlins consist of a buff, sandy, calcareous (limy) till carried from southeastern Manitoba by the Wadena lobe ice. The Wadena drumlins, like other drumlins, are elliptical hills of unstratified glacial material, their longer axes parallel to the direction of ice movement. Their higher and steeper ends are located upglacier; their lower, more sloping ends are located downglacier. Some drumlins may have formed when old glacial deposits were overrun and elongated by younger glaciers. The origin of many, however, is under debate.

Whatever their origin, drumlin fields exist elsewhere in Minnesota and the world. The Toimi drumlins are seen northwest of Duluth, the Pierz drumlins southeast of Little Falls, the Brainerd drumlins near Brainerd. Drumlins are found elsewhere in North America: near Rochester, New York; Halifax, Nova Scotia; and Madison, Wisconsin.

Balsamlund Church on the top of a drumlin near Aldrich.

A portion of the Wadena drumlin field from the USGS Brainerd
1:250,000, 1953 (revised 1975) map.

38 Headwaters of the Mississippi

Lake Itasca, Itasca State Park

COUNTY: **Clearwater**
NEAREST TOWN: **Lake Itasca**
OWNERSHIP: **State of Minnesota**
USGS TOPOGRAPHIC MAP: **Lake Itasca, 7½',**
1972

The Mississippi River officially begins its 2492-mile journey to the Gulf of Mexico at Lake Itasca in the high morainal hills of northwestern West Central Minnesota. The Mississippi is North America's largest and longest river, draining all or part of 31 states and two Canadian provinces. It is the third longest river system in the world. Rivers are major geologic, geographic, political, and social entities. Their place of origin is always of interest.

Lake Itasca is located in southeastern Clearwater County. It is surrounded by Itasca State Park, which also extends into neighboring Becker and Hubbard counties. The park is located approximately 30 miles northwest of Walker and 20 miles north of Park Rapids. From Park Rapids follow U.S. Highway 71 northward for approximately 20 miles to its intersection with Minnesota Highway 200. Continue north on Minnesota Highway 200 for 6.5 miles to the park entrance. Enter the park and stop at the information center. Spend time within the center studying its excellent displays and maps. Then follow the short path to the lake and the official headwaters of the Mississippi River. The remainder of the park may be thoroughly explored by automobile and foot—there are winding park roads and 22 hiking trails. There is a 100-foot-tall observation tower and a wilderness sanctuary. There are campgrounds and numerous other park amenities. This is Minnesota's oldest and perhaps best-known park. For further information write: Park Manager, Itasca State Park, Lake Itasca, Minnesota 56460. Phone: (218) 266-3654.

The Mississippi River officially begins in Lake Itasca, 1475 feet above sea level. It leaves the north end of this lake as a small stream less than 15 feet across and two feet deep. Even a child can thrown a stone across the stream, wade across it, or jump across it on stepping stones. The true headwaters of this river, however, exist somewhere in the many tributaries which flow into Lake Itasca from higher elevations. There are numerous isolated hills within this park which rise to elevations above 1600 feet. Among them is Alton Heights at 1675 feet and Ockerson Heights at 1665 feet.

Lake Itasca lies within the irregular knob and kettle landscape of the Itasca moraine. The moraine was deposited by the Wadena lobe, which melted from this region less than 20,000 years ago. The melting glacier left behind irregular piles of glacial till and outwash. Within the moraine and Itasca State Park are hills and holes, kames, and an esker. Buried melting ice blocks produced depressions in the landscape that filled with water and became lakes. Lakes Itasca, Alcon, and Mary are all ice-block lakes, localized within the channel of a buried bedrock valley.

Itasca State Park, covering approximately 32,000 acres, was established in 1891 to protect Lake Itasca, the headwaters of the Mississippi River, and the surrounding remnant stands of virgin red and white pine. The irregular landscape of the park also supports a great variety of other vegetation—marsh, thicket, bog, and hardwood forest. The park has been inhabited by man for at least 8000 years. First there were nomadic people here, then large permanent settlements. In 1832 Henry Rowe Schoolcraft reached Lake Itasca, named the lake—coining the word *itasca* from two Latin words *veritas caput*, which mean "true head,"—and called the lake the source of the Mississippi. Join these people of the past, numerous present-day university students, and many others to explore the park's hills and lakes, forests and marshes.

A portion of Lake Itasca and Itasca State Park, showing the source of the Mississippi River.

Lake Itasca, the source of the Mississippi River, Itasca State Park.

39 Chase Point Esker

Scenic State Park

COUNTY: **Itasca**
NEAREST TOWN: **Bigfork**
OWNERSHIP: **State of Minnesota**
USGS TOPOGRAPHIC MAP: **Coon Lake, 7½′, 1970**

Chase Point, a long, narrow, forested ridge separating Sandwick and Coon lakes, is the outstanding geologic feature of Scenic State Park. Eskers in general, and Chase Point in particular, are one of Minnesota's most unusual and intriguing glacial features. They are winding ridges of stratified sand and gravel which have been deposited in the beds of subglacial streams. Chase Point esker, besides being of geologic interest, is a curious fairyland sort of place, steep sided and scenic. An easy hiking trail runs along its 60- to 70-foot-high crest amidst a virgin forest of stately Norway pines.

Scenic State Park is located in northeastern Itasca County, approximately 45 miles northwest of Hibbing. It is located along Itasca County Road 7, seven miles east of Bigfork. Turn north into the park and follow the park road approximately 0.8 mile past the park headquarters to the Chase Point campground. Walk down to the shore there and look eastward across Coon Lake to the steep, wooded shore of Chase Point. Return to the trail head, 0.5 mile north of the park headquarters, and walk to the esker. The level, mile-long hike to the end of Chase Point esker provides many vistas of both Coon and Sandwick lakes and a journey through a pine forest which also contains northern white cedar, quaking aspen, and balsam fir. For more information on this park write: Manager, Scenic State Park, Bigfork, Minnesota 56628.

Scenic State Park, established in 1921, covers approximately 2000 acres and protects the virgin pine shorelines of Coon and Sandwick lakes. Glaciers melting from this region less than 10,000 years ago left depressions, ridges, numerous hills, and one magnificent esker with bordering esker troughs.

People always like eskers. They never seem quite real or natural, these high sinuous ridges which wind through the countryside. But they are natural. They are the inverted stream channels of subglacial rivers, which over time have left their bed loads as mounds of sand and gravel in tunnels of the glacial ice. As the ice melted, these mounds were left as ridges. Chase Point is one of these mysterious eskers, and it is even more wonderful and mysterious than most because it is bordered by two lakes, ends in the middle of a lake, and is covered with large red and white pines.

The lakes, Coon and Sandwick, alongside Chase Point have formed within esker troughs, depressions apparently formed because of lingering stagnant ice blocks on either side of an esker. Such esker troughs may occur on either flank of a single esker, or they may occur within a braided system of eskers. They are elongate in the direction of an esker and parallel to it. Most eskers, however, do not have bordering troughs.

Within Scenic State Park are many other glacial features, including kames and ice-block lakes. Throughout this entire morainal region—the Chippewa National Forest and portions of Bowstring and George Washington state forests— are almost innumerable other kames and ice-block lakes. There are also other eskers. However, since most of this area is heavily wooded and has poor access, Chase Point and Scenic State Park are particularly outstanding.

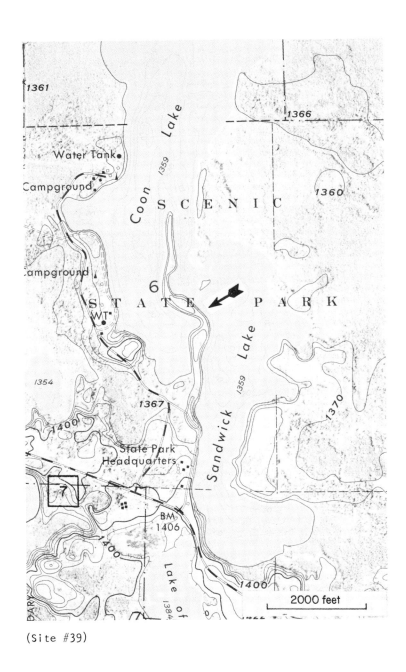

Within the map:

1361

1366

Water Tank●

1359

1360

Coon Lake

Campground

S C E N I C

ampground

6

S T A T E   P A R K

WT

Sandwick Lake

1359

1354

1370

1367

1400

State Park
Headquarters●

7

BM
1406

1400

Lake of

1400

1384

2000 feet

Trail along the top of Chase Point esker.

Mississippi River Meanders

Aitkin County

COUNTY: **Aitkin**
NEAREST TOWN: **Jacobson**
OWNERSHIP: **Aitkin County**
USGS TOPOGRAPHIC MAP: **Jacobson, 7½',
1970**

Rivers and streams are some of the most powerful geologic agents. In some places they wear away rock and carve out large valleys. In other places they wander slowly back and forth across gentle countryside, depositing sands, silts, and clays which they have picked up elsewhere. Rivers may be clear and boiling or dark and sluggish—or they may be both in different places and at different times. The Mississippi River between Grand Rapids and Aitkin is a slow, winding stream which meanders across a low, sandy glacial lake plain. The river twists and turns in broad curves known as meanders, constantly adding new curves and abandoning others. The abandoned curves slowly fill with sediments and become overgrown: the meanders become meander scars. Meanders and meander scars are present everywhere between Grand Rapids and Aitkin.

Perhaps the best place to examine this meandering situation is at the Aitkin County Mississippi River and Boat Landing. This park is located approximately 1.5 miles northwest of Jacobson. Follow Minnesota Highway 200 for 2.0 miles west from Jacobson. Turn north on Aitkin County Road 10 and proceed 0.5 mile to the marked access road. Follow this road 1.7 miles east to the river. The access is located on a large meander. Picnic sites are on the top of the cutbank. The landing is located near the slip-off slope. Meander scars may be seen in the woods to the south.

40

The Mississippi River in southern Itasca and northern Aitkin counties is typical of meandering streams everywhere. Wherever streams cross level, low-lying, easily eroded countryside they swing back and forth forming and reforming wide meanders. They constantly change course over space and time. This situation, evident on the ground, is particularly striking on a topographic map.

No one is exactly sure why meanders begin to form, but once begun they are constantly maintained. Water flowing downstream clings to the outer side of a bend where it is thrown by centrifugal force. Water then leaves the bend on a tangent crossing to the opposite bank and enters the next bend downstream. The steep outside bank, or cutbank, of each bend is constantly undermined. The inside, convex side, or slip-off slope, of each meander is a constant site of deposition. Consequently, the meanders continue to enlarge and migrate across the land surface. The stream loops and curls extravagantly. Not uncommonly, however, the meanders become enlarged and exaggerated to such a degree that the stream simply cuts through the narrowing point between the meanders and forms a new direct channel. The abandoned meander then becomes a meander scar. This process happens over and over again wherever streams flow through gentle, easily eroded countryside. The Mississippi River at this site is just such a stream.

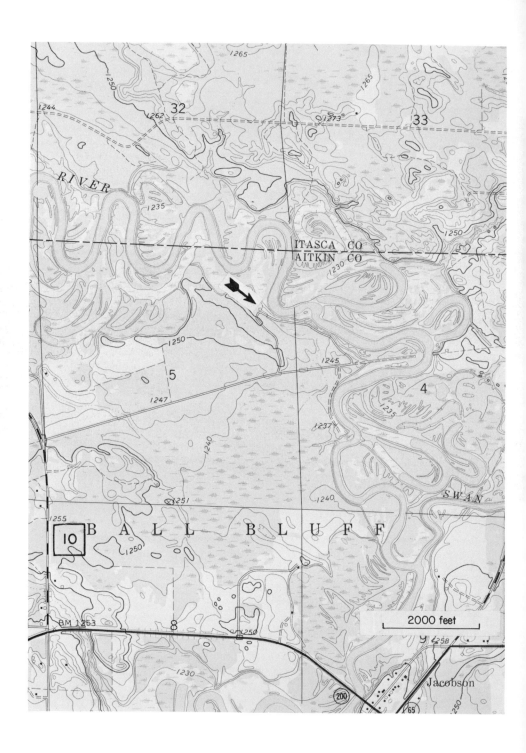

32

33

RIVER

1265

1250

1244

1262

1373

1265

1235

ITASCA CO
AITKIN CO

1250

1230

1250

5

1247

1250

1245

4

1235

1240

1237

1251

SWAN

1240

1255

10 B A L L   B L U F F

1250

1250

2000 feet

BM 1253

8

1250

9 1258

1230

Jacobson

200

65

1258

Meander on the Mississippi River, Aitkin County.

41 Bog Succession

Aitkin County

COUNTY: **Aitkin**
NEAREST TOWN: **Ball Bluff**
OWNERSHIP: **State of Minnesota**
USGS TOPOGRAPHIC MAPS: **Ball Bluff, 7½',
1970; Vanduse Lake, 7½', 1970**

Minnesota has many wetlands, wetlands of all shapes and all sizes. In fact, wetlands cover 35,111 square miles—22,471,200 acres (George Carlson, 1982, oral communication)—of an 84,068-square-mile state. Wetlands are found in the northern part of the state mostly as muskeg bogs, in the central part as spruce and tamarack swamps, and in the south as cattail marshes. The wetlands have often formed in old lake basins through vegetation growth, sediment accumulation, and time. This change from open water to vegetated wetland is called bog succession. One of the more interesting of these innumerable wetlands is a small tamarack-fringed marsh in northeastern Aitkin County. This marsh is indistinguishable from thousands of others except that contractors tried for years, ultimately unsuccessfully, to build a road across its center.

This particular wetland is located approximately four miles east of Minnesota Highway 65 between Jacobson and McGregor. The route to this site is somewhat devious. Follow Minnesota Highway 65 for 4.1 miles south of Jacobson or 25.7 miles north of McGregor. Turn east off the highway onto Aitkin County Road 65. Follow that gravel road as it winds southward around Black Face Lake and alongside small hills and swamps. Continue this winding route for 6.1 miles. At this point, the road makes a sudden, sharp turn to the east. This is the northern end of an old corduroy road which once crossed the wetland south of here.

Walk carefully along the old corduroy road 0.1 mile through alder thicket and sedge to open water.

This is a short, level, but dangerous walk. Open water exists under the corduroy roadbed and sedge mat. It is extremely difficult to get out of a broken mat. Do not follow this trail beyond the point of better judgment. If a view of open water is not obtained, simply study the included topographic map and aerial photograph.

Return to Minnesota Highway 65 either by the route followed to this site or, if the weather is dry and the road good, by following Aitkin County Road 65 southward 2.5 miles to its intersection with Aitkin County Road 14. Turn west on Aitkin County Road 14 and proceed 1.5 miles back to Minnesota Highway 65.

Most Minnesota wetlands have formed on glacial lake plains, in ice-block depressions, or simply within the lower portions of an irregular morainal landscape. Sediments of all kinds have turned lakes into wetlands. Often vegetation has grown so quickly over the open water that the centers of these depressions have vast sphagnum mats supporting various sedges, spruce, and tamarack trees. These floating mats are dangerous but interesting places because of their unusual assemblage of plants and their place in the transition between an open-water lake and an entirely sediment-filled wetland.

Most Minnesota lakes evolve into wetlands. Very occasionally this process is turned around, with a wetland becoming a lake. Beaver damming, human damming, dredging, or road construction may reverse the natural evolution.

This particular wetland has progressed through several thousand years of the same evolution as most wetlands. It was once a lake, possibly formed in an ice-block basin within a buried river channel. It was eventually overgrown with sphagnum, sedges, spruce, tamarack, and alder trees. However, the elongate band of open water which now exists in the center of this marsh denotes a reversal of this standard evolutionary process.

The story runs that builders tried unsuccessfully for several years to construct a road across this wetland. They built a roadbed of corduroy (crosswise logs) and, as is often the case with wetlands, could not get the corduroy to remain in place. Each log would tilt individually and ruin the roadbed. Instead of choosing a new route or continuing to build corduroy in the standard manner, the builders tied the logs together hoping they would then stay in place. Now, however, as the corduroy began to give way, the logs began to tilt as a unit instead of tilting individually. The corduroy road slowly tipped to the side,

turned on end, and finally slid down through the floating vegetation like a listing, tilting, and sinking ship. The road slid into the open water and disappeared.

The route across the wetland was abandoned. The road was rerouted around its eastern end. Only a long, thin lake indicates where the corduroy road once was. The natural vegetational growth across open water has been reinitiated.

The natural process of the filling in of lake basins must progress much farther than it has here before road construction is an easy, successful business. Geologic and biologic processes take time; man must not lose that perspective.

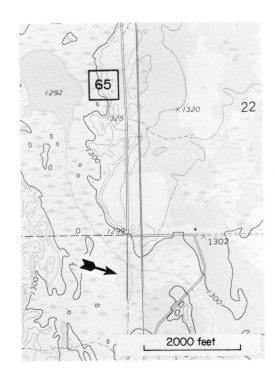

2000 feet

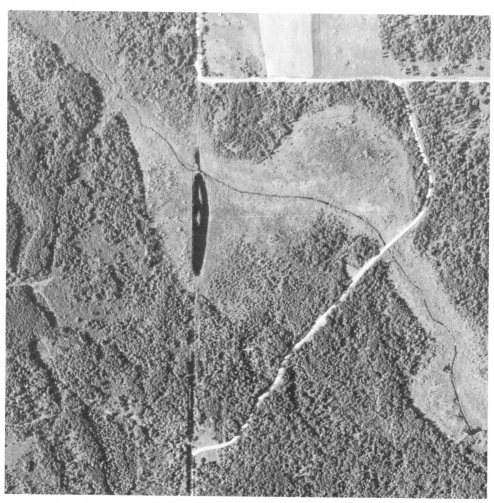

Aerial photograph of Site #41. Note the trees growing on higher elevations, the smaller wetland vegetation growing on lower elevations, and the elongate bank of open water marking the abandoned route of Aitkin County Road 65. Photograph courtesy of the Agricultural Stabilization and Conservation Service, U.S. Department of Agriculture.

Path of corduroy road through tamarack-fringed marsh, Aitkin County.

42 Mille Lacs Lake Ice Ramparts

Aitkin County

COUNTY: **Aitkin**
NEAREST TOWN: **Wealthwood**
OWNERSHIP: **State of Minnesota**
USGS TOPOGRAPHIC MAP: **Wealthwood, 7½', 1973**

A series of parallel sand ridges border the north side of Mille Lacs Lake. These ridges, known as ice ramparts, range in height to 25 feet. They were formed by the push and shove of lake ice. The higher ridges are covered with elm and sugar maple, the lower ridges with alder and birch. Swamps and occasional streams occur between the ridges. These ridges and their distinctive vegetation are easily seen along Minnesota Highway 18.

The largest ice rampart is seen just east of U.S. Highway 169 on Minnesota Highway 18. For approximately two miles east of this intersection, Minnesota Highway 18 follows along the top of this rampart. The highway then turns slightly away from the lake and drops off this rampart. As the road begins to turn away from the lake, pull off the right-hand side into a small, undeveloped parking area. Walk down to the beach. Note how the ridge rises up from the shore. Return to the car and continue on to Malmo. Along this route the road will parallel and cross many other ice ramparts. Particularly visible are those near the town of Malmo, where people have cut the vegetation on these ridges and built their homes among them.

Ice ramparts form when lake ice pushes against lake shores, shoving the shore material into ridges. The ice push occurs for two reasons: 1) through expan-

sion of winter ice and 2) through the breakup and shove of spring ice. Winter ice expands because of normal ice-water behavior. Water expands when it freezes, but ice reacts to changing temperatures by expanding with warmth and contracting with cold. Therefore, when the weather is very cold, the lake ice contracts. Since it cannot pull away from the shore, large cracks develop within the ice. Open water fills these cracks, freezes, and adds more ice to the lake. When the temperature again rises, the ice expands and pushes against the shore. The shove of spring ice occurs during spring melt: the lake ice is broken up into large chunks, driven by the wind, and pushed against the shore.

Ice ramparts form along Minnesota lakes wherever the material bordering the lake is not too firm to push into ridges. The shape and size of the lake encourage winter ice expansion and catch prevailing spring winds. The ramparts may consist of sand, gravel, rocks, boulders, and organic material, all jumbled together. Water separates materials from one another, but ice cannot do this. Bars and beaches are stratified, or layered—ramparts are not. The tops of ice ramparts are undulating, whereas the tops of bars and beaches are smooth.

Other outstanding ice ramparts are seen at Big McDonald Lake (Site #36) and at North Long Lake (see Site #43). However, many West Central Minnesota lakes have ice ramparts. Watch for steep, narrow, often rock-filled ridges along their shores.

Since ice ramparts can only form directly along lake shores, why are there a whole series of these ramparts north of Mille Lacs Lake? The lake must have been higher in the past than it is now. Careful tracing of these ramparts has shown that Mille Lacs Lake was once 15 feet higher than at present. Its water-level change may have been due to changes in precipitation, evaporation, in-flow, or out-flow. The lake level has now been stabilized by gates, dams, and a floating bog on the Rum River.

Mille Lacs Lake is interesting in itself. This large, circular lake covers nearly 200 square miles and has a maximum depth of only 40 feet. The country north and east of the lake is relatively low and gentle. Along the west and south sides of the lake is an impressive belt of hummocky topography known as the Mille Lacs moraine. This moraine has dammed the lake, preventing the natural flowage of its waters to the southwest and flooding the low sandy land to the north. The moraine has produced this broad, shallow lake, a lake of ideal size and dimension for the development of ice ramparts.

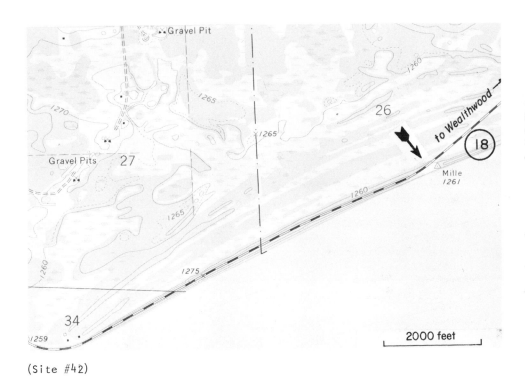

(Site #42)

Beach and bordering ice rampart on the north shore of Mille Lacs Lake.

Ice rampart along the north shore of Mille Lacs Lake.

Brainerd Pitted Outwash Plain

Crow Wing County

COUNTY: **Crow Wing**
NEAREST TOWN: **Nisswa**
OWNERSHIP: **Public roadway and public lake access**
USGS TOPOGRAPHIC MAP: **Gull Lake, 7½',
1973**

The nearly level sandy countryside near
Brainerd is pockmarked with hundreds
of rounded lakes and marshes. This
type of country is known as a pitted
outwash plain and has formed at the
front of a receding glacier. This sand
and lake country is a favorite of vaca-
tioning Minnesotans. The lakes are
shallow, warm, and clear. Their bottoms and shores are gentle and sandy.
The land is excellent for hiking and
horseback riding trails. Summer camps
and summer cottages abound. This pitted sand country is particularly evident
near Nisswa and Merrifield.

North Long Lake, Round Lake, and
Ruth Lake are excellent, accessible,
classic examples of ice-block basins in
glacial outwash. These three lakes and
numerous others are located approximately six miles northwest of Brainerd
on Minnesota Highway 371. The
highway skirts along the west shores of
North Long and Round lakes. It runs
approximately 1.5 miles east of Ruth
Lake. Stop at the public access on the
northwest side of North Long Lake,
where there is a picnic table and an excellent view of the lake. Note the low
sandy shores and bordering ice rampart
(see Site #42). Numerous rushes growing within the lake indicate its minimal
depth. After leaving this public access,
turn south on Minnesota Highway 371.
Drive for 0.7 mile and turn right on
Crow Wing County Road 126 (Green
Gables Road). Drive west for 1.5 miles

to Ruth Lake. Ruth Lake is a much
smaller, more understandable, and less
complex ice-block lake than the other
two. View this lake from the county
road.

43

Pitted outwash plains form at the front
of receding glaciers where glacial
meltwaters have spread out, deposited
their loads of sand and gravel, and
buried large blocks of ice. These ice
remnants have subsequently melted and
left depressions, pits in an otherwise
sandy, level landscape. The ice blocks
vary tremendously in size. The resulting
depressions range from feet to miles
across.

Outwash plains are common within
Minnesota and are recognized by their
low, minimally rolling, sandy landscape, a landscape characterized by
swells and swales. Outwash plains are
often pitted to some degree by ice-block
depressions and lakes, but not usually to
the degree seen near Brainerd. Here
ice-block depressions exist everywhere.
It is noteworthy that 80% to 85% of the
lakes in Minnesota have formed within
ice-block depressions (Zumberge, 1952,
p. 83), though not all within sandy
outwash.

The underlying sand of outwash
plains is very permeable, allowing
water to flow readily from one place to
another and producing a nearly level
water table. The lake elevations within
an outwash plain thus tend to be very
similar to one another. For example,
the surface elevation of Round Lake is
1194 feet, West Long Lake 1197 feet,
and Ruth Lake 1199 feet. Neighboring
Gull Lake has a water level of 1194
feet, and Moberg Lake, between West
Long and Ruth lakes, has an elevation
of 1196 feet. In contrast, the water
level of adjacent ice-block lakes within
glacial till is often highly variable: till
has a great deal of clay in it and water
cannot flow readily from one lake basin
to another. This situation is seen near
Lake Minnetonka (Site #32). There the
surface elevation of neighboring lakes
often has a difference of 20 to 30 feet.

The sandy soils of outwash plains cannot support the lush vegetation of many other soils and landscapes in Minnesota. They are coarse textured and droughty, much in contrast to the often fine and moisture-retentive soils of other portions of the state. The Brainerd outwash plain is no exception. The somewhat higher areas of the plain are dominated by jack pine, northern pin oak, and occasionally red pine. The lower areas, closer to the water table, support occasional paper birch and ash.

Elsewhere in this region, under the same climatic conditions but with far heavier and more moisture-retentive soils, elm, maple, basswood, red oak, and green ash predominate.

Before leaving the Brainerd area, look carefully once more at the gentle swell and swale and pitted topography of this outwash plain. Contrast this landscape with the mountainous highlands near Pigeon Point (Site #9), the sink-riddled fields near Wykoff (Site #25), the drumlin-strewn country near Wadena

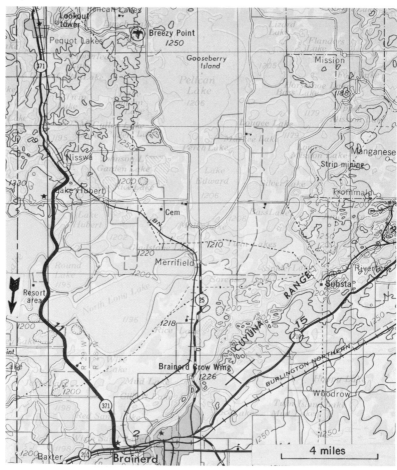

A portion of the Brainerd outwash plain showing numerous ice-block lakes, from the USGS Brainerd 1:250,000, 1953 (revised 1975) map.

(Site #25), and the knobs and kettles near Lake Itasca (Site #38). This pitted outwash plain is just one of the many variations of Minnesota's diverse land surface.

Ruth Lake, an ice-block lake in the Brainerd outwash plain.

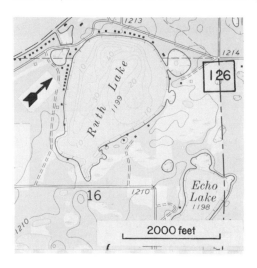

44 Ripley Esker

Morrison County

COUNTY: **Morrison**
NEAREST TOWN: **Fort Ripley**
OWNERSHIP: **The Nature Conservancy**
USGS TOPOGRAPHIC MAPS: **Fort Ripley,
7½', 1956; Belle Prairie, 7½', 1956**

Eskers are long, narrow, sinuous ridges which wind across the landscape. They are composed of stratified sands and gravels that have been laid down by subglacial streams. The Ripley esker, widely illustrated in introductory geology texts, is 10 to 60 feet high, 225 to 250 feet across, and nearly seven miles long. It winds across a gently rolling plain of glacial till and was formed approximately 20,500 years ago when continental glaciers covered this part of central Minnesota (Searle and Heitlinger, 1980, p. 38). Native prairie and forest vegetation have been preserved on this steep-sided landform, and from its top are panoramas of the surrounding countryside.

The Ripley esker is located in northern Morrison County, approximately eight miles north of Little Falls. Follow Minnesota Highway 371 north from Little Falls for approximately seven miles to County Road 48. Turn eastward on County Road 48 and travel 0.9 mile to County Road 282. Turn northward on this gravel road and proceed 1.3 miles to the Ripley esker. The road cuts through the esker: on the west side is an overgrown gravel pit (a common use for eskers); on the east side is a Nature Conservancy preserve. Park along the road just north of the esker. Follow the Nature Conservancy trail southward onto the esker and along its crest. Follow the Nature Conservancy trails and follow their rules: no dogs, no picnics, no picking or removal of plants or natural objects of any sort, no motor-ized vehicles. Take special care of these surroundings.

Eskers are the most remarkable form of stratified drift. They range in height from five feet to 150 feet, in breadth from five feet to more than 600 feet, in length from less than 300 feet to more than 250 miles. Their sides are generally steep, and their tops may be either smooth or broadly hummocky. Their sinuous nature approximates that of normal streams. Many have tributaries and some have distributaries. Most eskers occur in regions of rather low relief and trend parallel to the direction of the latest glacial flow (Flint, 1957, p. 153). Esker gradients are gentle but not necessarily continuous. An esker may climb up a valley and pass over a divide. Some eskers connect downstream to fans or deltas. Others end in kames.

Eskers occur in many places throughout Minnesota, North America, and Scandinavia. Most Minnesota eskers, however, are not accessible, and many have not been mapped. Some of the state's well-known eskers include Chase Point in Scenic State Park (Site #39), Schoolcraft Ridge in Itasca State Park, the Cross Lake esker near Pine City, the St. Rosa esker near St. Rosa, and the Bridgewater esker near Faribault. Perhaps America's most famous eskers are those in southern Maine, many of which run for more than 20 miles. Hundreds, perhaps thousands of eskers occur in a radial fashion surrounding Hudson Bay; one of these is perhaps the world's longest esker.

The Ripley esker is noteworthy not only as an esker but also for the dramatic contrast between vegetative communities on its north and south sides. The cooler, moister northern side supports plants typical of the northern forest: northern pin oak, quaking aspen, paper birch, hazel brush, Solomon's seal, large-leaved aster, and black snakeroot. The warmer, drier southern side supports prairie and savannah species such as big and little bluestem, leadplant, spiderwort, prairie onion, blazing star, hoary puccoon, and bur oak. The diversity of vegetation supports a diversity of insects and birds.

Ripley esker, near Fort Ripley.

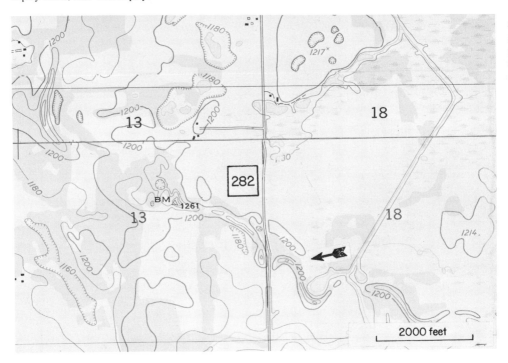

45 St. Cloud Granite

Cold Spring Granite Quarry, Rockville

COUNTY: **Stearns**
NEAREST TOWN: **Rockville**
OWNERSHIP: **Cold Spring Granite Company**
USGS TOPOGRAPHIC MAP: **Rockville, 7½',**
1967

The striking pink, red, and gray granite of the St. Cloud area is noteworthy because of its economic importance and widespread use. These rocks, similar to those found in Northeastern Minnesota (see Sites #11 and #17), cooled deep within the earth's crust during the Proterozoic, approximately 1.6 billion years ago. The granite has been used principally for building and monument stone; it has been shipped to nearly every state and to many foreign countries. It is a major building component of the cathedral in St. Paul, the Tribune Tower in Chicago, and the Louisiana State Capitol in Baton Rouge (Schwartz and Thiel, 1954, p. 269). The St. Cloud granite can be cut and polished for a high gloss or broken and chiseled for a rough-textured appearance. It may be gray and somber or pink and lively. The Cold Spring Company's Rockville quarry is one of the state's largest producers of the St. Cloud granite.

Rockville is located 12 miles southwest of St. Cloud along Minnesota Highway 23. The Rockville quarry is located in the northeastern corner of town, immediately north of the highway. The quarry is privately owned and heavily fenced. However, there is an excellent vantage point for the entire operation from a small public road along the fence's east side.

Granites crop out in Minnesota near St. Cloud, the Giants Range, the border lakes, Mille Lacs, and in the Minnesota River valley. These rocks vary in color, composition, and precise age, but all are composed primarily of quartz and feldspar, are medium or coarse grained, and are of Precambrian age. The granites have been used, among other things, for driveway rock, steel pickling tanks, and stone walls. The color of Minnesota's granites ranges from dark gray to almost white, from red to pink, brown, blue, and green.

Granite quarrying began in Minnesota around 1868 near Sauk Rapids. The Cold Spring Granite Company, one of the United States' largest granite producers, began operation in Rockville in 1889. The company presently owns 25 quarries in eight states and Canada. The granite at this particular quarry is considered one of the best in the Cold Spring Granite Company's family of quarries (Ted Kresbach, 1982, oral communication). The color of the rock in this quarry grades from pink to gray: the dominant minerals are quartz and feldspar and the minor minerals are biotite, hornblende, and magnetite. The rock is classed as a porphyritic quartz monzonite. There are large crystals of feldspar imbedded in a background of medium-crystalled quartz and feldspar. The rock from this quarry is used in all the Cold Spring Granite Company's divisions—building work, monument work, mausoleum and cemetery feature work, and industrial use. It is most widely used in their structural department (Ibid.).

Granite is a favorite building material because it resists weather and stains. It does not fade or deteriorate and is practically maintenance free. The existence of granite exposures scattered throughout Minnesota, and virtually unaltered for tens of millions of years, attests to its durability.

St. Cloud Granite at the Rockville granite quarry, Rockville.

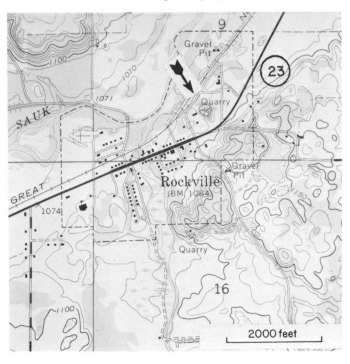

Black spruce trees in the patterned peatland, near Waskish, Northwestern Minnesota.

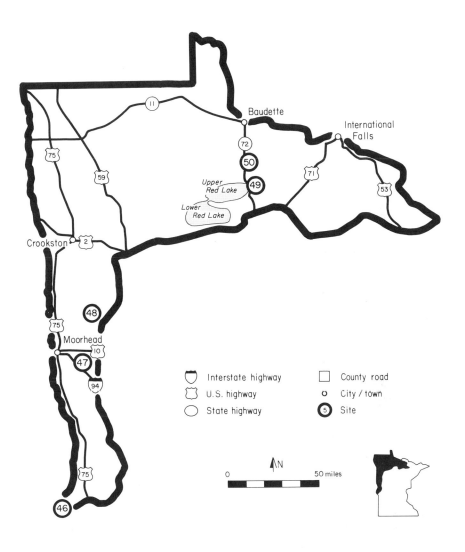

Baudette

International
Falls

Upper
Red Lake

Lower
Red Lake

Crookston

Moorhead

	Interstate highway		County road
	U.S. highway	○	City / town
	State highway	⑤	Site

0   50 miles

V   Northwestern Minnesota

Glacial Lake Agassiz

Northwestern Minnesota is today an almost flat, virtually lakeless region. Ten thousand years ago, however, it was covered by North America's largest ice-margin lake, Glacial Lake Agassiz—a lake larger than all the present Great Lakes combined. Since that time and the lake's drainage, bluestem prairie has grown in the western portion of this region and conifer bog in the east. In recent years the prairie has given way to the intense cultivation of wheat, rye, oats, sugar beets, barley, flax, and potatoes. To the east, in Lake of the Woods and Koochiching counties, the country remains a wetland of larch, spruce, cedar, sedge, heath, and sphagnum moss. Throughout the entire region are rich organic and clay soils, soils which have developed on lake-deposited sediments. These soils and lake deposits often overlie several hundred feet of glacial drift, which in turn overlies rocks of varying age and composition. Nowhere is the bedrock exposed. Only deep wells and subsurface geophysical work attest to its presence and composition.

Northwestern Minnesota is bounded by low sand, gravel, and boulder ridges—abandoned beaches of Glacial Lake Agassiz. To the east and south of these beaches is the high, rugged, wooded, morainal land of West Central Minnesota, a land strewn with small lakes. The margin of Glacial Lake Agassiz and thus the borders of Northwestern Minnesota can be easily found by noting the edge of Minnesota's lake country.

The old shore of Glacial Lake Agassiz may be traced from Browns Valley northward along the valley of the Red River to Mentor, approximately 25 miles east-southeast of Crookston. From here the shore turns abruptly eastward, passes just south of Lower Red Lake, and continues east as far as the Little Fork River in St. Louis County. The shore then turns northward again and enters Canada east of Lake of the Woods (Schwartz and Thiel, 1954, p. 252). Much of this eastward extension, known as the Big Bog, was occupied by the lake only in its earlier stages (Wright, *in* Sims and Morey, 1972, p. 576).

Lake Agassiz formed as the last glacier retreated from Northwestern Minnesota. As the ice melted it left behind a series of moraines, high irregular piles of glacial drift. One of these moraines, the Big Stone moraine, formed on the continental divide just north of Browns Valley (Matsch and Wright, 1966, p. 121). As the glacier retreated northward from this moraine, its meltwaters ponded, their drainage to the south blocked by the high land and their natural drainage to the north blocked by the remaining ice. Glacial Lake Agassiz was born. As the ice continued to melt, the lake continued to grow. Glacial Lake Agassiz eventually covered parts of Minnesota, South Dakota, North Dakota, Saskatchewan, Manitoba, and Ontario—a region of more than 110,000 square miles. This lake was more than 700 miles from its southern tip in western Minnesota to its northern tip near Hudson Bay. It extended more than 600 miles northwestward from Lake of the Woods to the Saskatchewan River. Along its northern border it was perhaps 600 to 700 feet deep (Schwartz and Thiel, 1954, p. 257).

Approximately 12,000 years ago (Matsch and Wright, 1966, p. 137) the lake overflowed the Big Stone moraine at Browns Valley, cut an outlet channel, and flowed southeastward as Glacial River Warren. This large river cut the deep, broad valley now occupied by the Minnesota River. As the ice continued to melt, the lake continued to enlarge and the outlet channel to deepen. Periodically the lake level stabilized, and beaches formed along its shores. These beaches remain today as rocky or sandy ridges in an otherwise level, silty countryside.

By approximately 9200 years ago the glaciers had melted far enough to the north that lower outlets were uncovered (Ibid., p. 128). Glacial River Warren was beheaded. Glacial Lake Agassiz rapidly diminished.

Today only a few undrained depressions remain of this once enormous lake: Upper Red Lake and Lower Red Lake, Lake of the Woods, and Lake Winnipeg (Schwartz and Thiel, 1954, p. 258). But the rich lake-laid soils remain, as do the flat, seemingly endless lake bottom land and the numerous parallel beach ridges. And in the spring when flood waters cover the entire Red River valley, it is not so difficult to imagine that once all of Northwestern Minnesota was covered by North America's largest glacial lake.

Glacial Lake Agassiz plain, near Fargo-Moorhead.

Traverse Gap

Browns Valley

COUNTY: **Big Stone**
NEAREST TOWN: **Browns Valley**
OWNERSHIP: **Public roadway**
USGS TOPOGRAPHIC MAP: **Browns Valley,
7½', 1971**

Traverse Gap is the point at which the waters of Glacial Lake Agassiz broke through the continental divide and began to drain southeastward across central Minnesota. Water poured through this limited outlet for approximately 3000 years, creating an enormous gap, or channel. Today this channel is approximately one mile across and 130 feet deep. It is located near Browns Valley on the Minnesota–South Dakota border between the heads of Big Stone Lake and Lake Traverse. Today it is occupied by the diminutive Little Minnesota River. The maximum elevation of the valley floor is 987 feet, still the lowest point on the continental divide in this vicinity.

An excellent view of this ancient stream channel with its flanking terraces is obtained from the west side of Minnesota Highway 28, approximately 2.5 miles southeast of Browns Valley. The highway runs southeastward from Browns Valley along the channel and terraces for several miles, then turns abruptly eastward and climbs onto the upland. Park safely off the roadway in the southwestern corner of section 3, just before the turn. This is an excellent vantage point for the entire length and width of Traverse Gap: from Lake Traverse and Browns Valley to Big Stone Lake, from Minnesota into South Dakota.

This vantage point is located on a pronounced stream terrace, an old valley floor. Note the flattened step in the

general valley configuration and the numerous boulders in the nearby field. As Glacial River Warren broke through the continental divide, broke through the Big Stone moraine, it carried all the small and medium-sized glacial materials downstream—only the large boulders were left as a lag deposit on the channel floor. This boulder-strewn terrace, at an elevation of 1045 feet, indicates the highest stillstand of Glacial Lake Agassiz, the Herman stage: the terrace is correlative with the Herman beach (see Site #48).

Renewed downcutting of the Traverse Gap and consequent diminishment of Glacial Lake Agassiz caused the formation of lower terraces and beaches. A second terrace occurs in this vicinity. This lower terrace, also boulder covered, is at an elevation of 1000 feet and may be correlative with the Tintah beach (INQUA, 1965, p. 36).

Traverse Gap was occupied by the powerful Glacial River Warren from approximately 12,000 to 9200 years ago (Matsch and Wright, 1966, p. 133). After that time glaciers had melted enough that lower outlets were uncovered to the north and east. Glacial River Warren ceased to exist. Waters north of Browns Valley again flowed to the Arctic and those south of Browns Valley again flowed to the Gulf of Mexico. The large channel that was formed all the way across central Minnesota by the Glacial River Warren no longer served as a drainageway for North America's largest glacial lake. The river, now known as the Minnesota River, was fed only by small tributary streams.

Since the diversion northward of Glacial Lake Agassiz, the floor of this ancient channel has slowly filled with the sediments of lakes and streams; the relatively small Minnesota River could no longer carry away all the river-borne materials brought into its large channel. Small tributary streams flowed into this large valley, deposited alluvial fans, and divided the valley floor into a series of

46

long, shallow lakes—Lake Traverse, Big Stone Lake, and Lac Qui Parle Lake, among others.

The Minnesota River valley today, occupied by alluvial fans, large shallow lakes, and a small, usually serene, silt-laden, winding river, is a far cry from its mighty water-filled, rock-floored

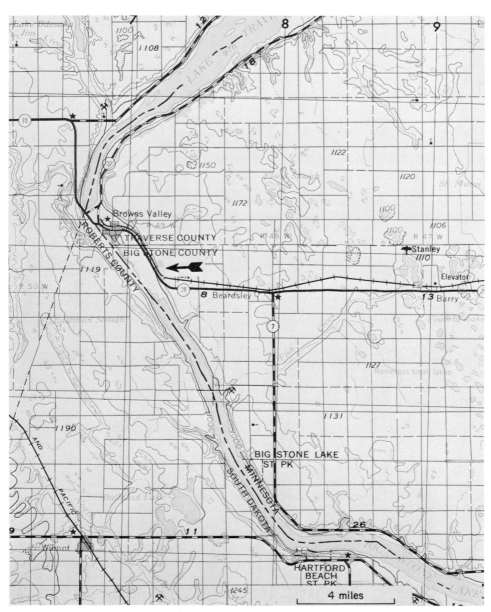

Traverse Gap between the heads of Big Stone Lake and Lake Traverse. The Minnesota River and the Red River of the North begin here. This map is a portion of the USGS Milbank 1:250,000, 1953 (revised 1975) map.

ancestor. The Traverse Gap is today marsh floored and pastured, again a dis- tant, subdued vision of a larger, turbulence-filled gorge.

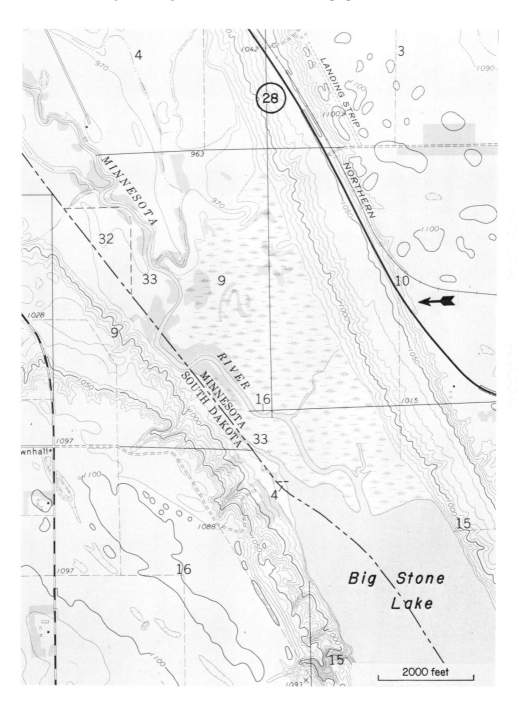

Boulder terrace, Traverse Gap and north end of Big Stone Lake, near Browns Valley.

Glacial Lake Agassiz Plain

Clay County

COUNTY: **Clay**
NEAREST TOWN: **Downer**
OWNERSHIP: **Public roadway**
USGS TOPOGRAPHIC MAP: **Glyndon South, 7½', 1964**

47

Fargo-Moorhead and the neighboring towns of Dilworth, Sabin, Glyndon, and Kragnes are built on the old Agassiz lake plain. Downer is built on an abandoned beach at the edge of the lake plain. Running through the center of this lake plain is the low-gradient, strongly meandering Red River of the North. Much of the Agassiz lake plain, once seemingly endless level prairie, is now just as seemingly endless cultivated farmland. Its local relief is generally less than 10 feet. The area between Sabin and Downer, southeast of Fargo-Moorhead, typifies well the almost level expanse of the ancient Glacial Lake Agassiz floor.

Approach Fargo-Moorhead from the southeast on Interstate Highway 94. The highway travels for miles through open, level countryside. Note the extreme flatness of this country by looking down the highway and sensing the roadways converging in the distance. Exit at the Sabin-Downer exit, Clay County Road 10, approximately eight miles from Moorhead. Cross the overpass, pull off the road, and look at the level land extending in all directions. Note that the land is cut into large, neat, regular fields and sections. Roads follow almost all the section lines. The highest part of the landscape is usually the roadway.

The lack of topographic diversity is the major feature of the Lake Agassiz plain, which defines Northwestern Minnesota and extends for thousands of square miles. Glacial Lake Agassiz covered this whole region for approximately 3000 years, from approximately 11,000 to 9000 years ago (see Introduction to Region V and Site #46). Streams and glaciers brought into this lake all types of rock material, which waves and currents moved about, piling on its shores and spreading out on its bottom. Over time the lake basin, formed on an irregular surface of glacial till and river-borne sands and gravels, became more regular and level. As the lake drained, waves smoothed out any remaining irregularities. The lake floor became a flat, nearly featureless plain.

Today not only does the topography of Northwestern Minnesota reflect this lacoustrine inheritance, but so also do the soils. The rich agricultural soils of the Red River valley are primarily mollisols. These organically rich, well-textured, moisture-retentive soils developed from silty lake bottom sediments and decaying prairie vegetation. To the east, in Beltrami and Koochiching counties, the organic histosols developed on the poorly drained conifer-, moss-, and heath-covered peatlands (Site #50). Today much of Northwestern Minnesota, once covered by an enormous glacial lake, is drained by the Red River of the North and its tributary streams. It is flat, easily tilled, agriculturally productive land, truly the gift of Glacial Lake Agassiz.

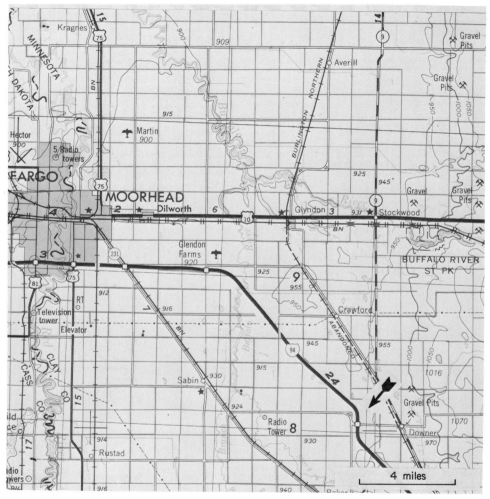

A portion of the Agassiz lake plain near Fargo-Moorhead, from the USGS Fargo 1:250,000, 1953 (revised 1975) map. Note the virtually flat land and regularly laid-out roads of the western portion of the map. The elevated land and gravel pits on the east side of the map indicate Glacial Lake Agassiz beaches.

Glacial Lake Agassiz plain near Sabin.

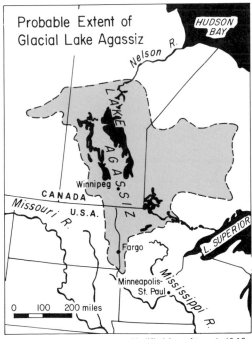

Probable Extent of
Glacial Lake Agassiz

HUDSON BAY

Nelson R.

LAKE AGASSIZ

Winnipeg

CANADA
U.S.A.

Missouri R.

Fargo

L. SUPERIOR

Minneapolis-
St. Paul

Mississippi R.

0   100   200 miles

Modified from Atwood, 1940

48 Glacial Lake Agassiz Beaches

Norman County

COUNTY: **Norman**
NEAREST TOWN: **Borup, Syre**
OWNERSHIP: **Public roadway, The Nature Conservancy**
USGS TOPOGRAPHIC MAPS: **Borup, 7½′, 1966; Ulen NW, 7½′, 1965; Syre, 7½′, 1965; Flom, 7½′, 1966**

As Glacial Lake Agassiz subsided, beaches were formed and left along its margins. There are four prominent beaches: the Herman at an elevation of approximately 1060 feet, the Norcross at 1040 feet, the Tintah at 1020 feet, and the Campbell at 980 feet (Matsch and Wright, 1966, pp. 122, 128). These beaches, named for the towns through which they pass, continued uninterrupted for hundreds of miles throughout Northwestern Minnesota. They mark the edge of the Glacial Lake Agassiz plain and the margin fo the higher morainal country to the east and south. In the western portion of this region the beaches are unforested, visible, and often the location of farms, gravel pits, and roads. To the east the ridges and surrounding land are heavily wooded. The beaches are composed of sand, gravel, cobbles, and boulders and may be marked either by a rise or a ridge. They are generally five to 25 feet high.

Borup is located at the intersections of Minnesota highways 9 and 113, 25 miles northeast of Moorhead. Begin at Borup and proceed east on Minnesota Highway 113. Drive 18 miles through the town of Syre, then turn northward on County Road 36 and proceed 1.8 miles to Frenchman's Bluff. For the first mile the land is level and cultivated, typical of the Glacial Lake Agassiz floor. For the next 4.5 miles the land rises imperceptibly eastward, still a portion of the old lake bed. In the next 0.2 mile, at mile 5.5, the road rises 25 feet, up the lowest but most pronounced beach. Between here and Syre, five more beaches are traversed (Searle and Heitlinger, 1980, p. 8). Each beach appears as a slight rise with a long, sweeping slope to the west and a comparatively level bench or terrace to the east. The road crosses the highest beach, the Herman beach, immediately west of the railroad track in Syre. The highway then leaves the lake bed and continues eastward into morainal country.

Four miles east of Syre turn north on Norman County Road 36. Proceed 1.3 miles to Frenchman's Bluff. Park on the east side of the road, cross the road, and climb the hill. The top of this bluff, a Nature Conservancy preserve, is 450 feet above the Glacial Lake Agassiz floor at Borup and 230 feet above the highest beach ridge near Syre. Look westward from this vantage point onto the open country of the Agassiz lake plain. Look northeastward into woody, hilly country of the Big Stone moraine.

Glacial Lake Agassiz beaches have been carbon dated as ranging in age from 11,700 to 9200 years (Matsch and Wright, 1966, p. 128). They correlate with the terraces at Traverse Gap (Site #46) and may be seen at many places throughout Northwestern Minnesota. Several other particularly noteworthy spots are: near Karlstad in the southeastern corner of Kittson County, within Buffalo River State Park near Moorhead, and near the town of Gemmell in southwestern Koochiching County.

To fully appreciate the Agassiz beaches, always approach them from the lake side. These small ridges or rises then appear topographically significant. If the beaches are approached from the land side, their slight elevational changes are lost in the comparison to the nearby hills.

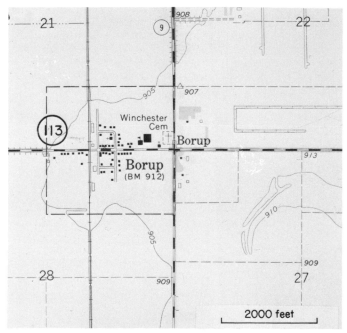

An Agassiz beach, between Borup and Syre.

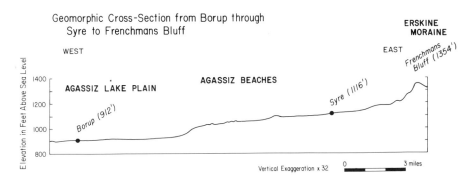

Geomorphic Cross-Section from Borup through Syre to Frenchmans Bluff

ERSKINE
MORAINE

WEST

EAST

Frenchmans
Bluff (1354')

Elevation in Feet Above Sea Level

1400

AGASSIZ LAKE PLAIN

AGASSIZ BEACHES

1200

Syre (1116')

Borup (912')

1000

800

Vertical Exaggeration x 32

0   3 miles

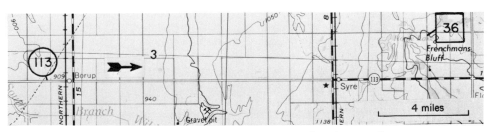

The route across the Agassiz beaches onto the Big Stone moraine, from Borup to Syre to
Frenchman's Bluff. This map is a portion of the USGS Grand Forks 1:250,000, 1952 (revised 1975) map.

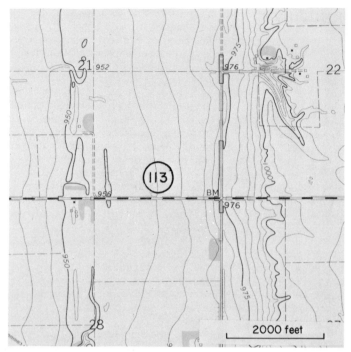

The flat Glacial Lake Agassiz plain surrounding Borup.

View of Agassiz beach, the slight rise in the distance, on Minnesota Highway 113, between Borup and Syre.

Red Lake Strandlines

Waskish

COUNTY: **Beltrami**
NEAREST TOWN: **Waskish**
OWNERSHIP: **State of Minnesota**
USGS TOPOGRAPHIC MAP: **Waskish, 7½′, 1973**

Along the eastern and southern shores of Upper Red Lake and especially in the vicinity of Waskish are long, low, parallel sand ridges. These are seen readily from the air or on a topographic map with a photographic base. They are far more difficult to see on the ground, but may be noted by walking across them and closely watching vegetational and elevational changes. These ridges are old beaches, or strandlines, formed when Red Lake stood at higher levels than today.

The town of Waskish, on Minnesota Highway 72 midway between Baudette and Blackduck on the eastern shore of Upper Red Lake, is built on these abandoned strandlines. In the center of town, on the east side of the highway, Waskish Baptist Church, a trailer home, and the Cove Cafe are built directly on one of these ridges. On the north edge of town, the Tamarac River parallels the ridges, cuts through them, and runs out to the lake. A forest service campground located immediately east of the road and south of the Tamarac River has been built on the beach ridges. A public access, across the beach ridges onto the present beach of Upper Red Lake, is located 0.3 mile south of the river. Park in the campground, then walk or drive to the public access and out to the lake.

Upper and Lower Red lakes have formed in a large, shallow depression left in the floor of Glacial Lake Agassiz. These lakes, along with Lake of the Woods and Lake Winnipeg,

are small, undrained portions of the once mighty Agassiz. Upper and Lower Red lakes are two large connected ovals separated by a long sandspit from the east. Abandoned strandlines on this point and elsewhere along the lake make it apparent that the lake level has dropped within the past several hundred or thousand years. Each ridge records momentarily stable levels of this continually diminishing lake. Today the lake has a maximum depth of 31 feet and covers 451 square miles. Today man has stabilized the level of Upper and Lower Red lakes at an elevation of 1175 feet; no longer will the paralleling strandlines continue to form.

Take a closer look at the strandlines. First examine them on the adjoining topographic map, then at the forest service campground, and then along the present lake shore. These ridges are parallel to one another, varying distances apart, slightly less than five feet high and 15 feet across. They are composed entirely of sand. The campsite in the far southwestern corner of the campground is on the crest of one of these ridges. This particular ridge parallels the highway and continues northward to the center of the campground, where it then turns east to the Tamarac River. Numerous other beaches occur in the woods between the campground and the lake.

Proceed to the public access on the low, sandy, present shore of Upper Red Lake. Walk to the shore, look out across the lake, and examine the present-day beach. This lake shore has probably looked somewhat like this for several thousand years—the whole countryside in this vicinity is low and sandy. After examining the beach, walk into the woods, east toward the highway, and across several beach ridges and intervening swales. Note that the vegetation of the ridges, or strandlines, is quite different from that of the swales. The ridges support balsam, fir, large-toothed aspen, oak, red pine, large-leaved aster, and bracken fern. The swales support willow, ash, alder, sedges, and sensitive fern.

It would be interesting to trace the strandlines around Upper and Lower Red lakes and to carbon date the wood buried within the strands. This information would tell how rapidly the lake levels had decreased and over what span of time. The information would also aid the speculation concerning man's ultimate success in stabilizing the lake levels.

Forest service campground at Waskish. Note the strandlines of earlier, higher levels of Upper Red Lake.

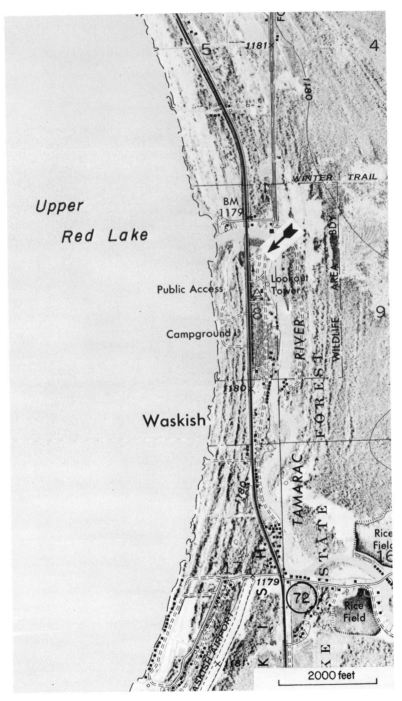

Upper
Red Lake

Public Access

Campground

Waskish

BM 1179

Lookout Tower

WINTER TRAIL

RIVER FOREST

WILDLIFE AREA

BDY

1181×

1180

1180

1180×

1179

72

TAMARAC STATE

WASKISH AIRPORT

1181

KE

Rice Field

Rice Field

2000 feet

(Site #49)

Low sandy shore of Upper Red Lake, Waskish.

Patterned Peatland

Beltrami County

COUNTY: **Beltrami**
NEAREST TOWN: **Waskish**
OWNERSHIP: **Public roadway**
USGS TOPOGRAPHIC MAP: **Ludlow Lookout Tower, 7½', 1973**

A vast wetland, developed on the eastern, poorly-drained portion of the Glacial Lake Agassiz plain, occupies much of Lake of the Woods, Roseau, Beltrami, and Koochiching counties. The whole region is underlain by peat, partially decomposed plant material, and is known as the Red Lake Peatland. Portions of the peatland show an unusual and striking patterning of islands, ridges, pools, and drains. These geomorphic features are strongly enhanced by vegetational differences. Patterned peatlands are found in only a few places of the world, and their origin is still enigmatic. Dr. H. E. Wright, Jr., and his colleagues at the University of Minnesota are currently studying the origin of this unusual patterning. This study is truly at the interface of geology and botany—the study of land and rock and the study of plants.

The only reasonably accessible place to view the patterned peatland is along Minnesota Highway 72 in northern Beltrami County, north of Waskish. This highway traverses the heart of these patterned peatlands and displays well their striking vegetational variations. However, the peatland is in a more natural state to the east of the road, since the raised roadbed has interrupted the drainage westward. The most representative stretch of the peatland is found beginning approximately 10 miles north of Waskish between mileposts 46 and 51. Along this stretch of the highway are patches of tamarack, black spruce, dwarf birch, leatherleaf, Labrador tea, blueberry, sedges, and sphagnum moss.

The Red Lake Peatland covers an area of approximately 450 square miles. It is uninterrupted by streams and uplands and is one of the largest continuous mires in the conterminous United States (Glaser, Wheeler, Gorham, and Wright, 1981, p. 576). Much of the peatland consists of a vast patterned complex of raised bogs and water tracks, of ovoid and teardrop-shaped islands, and of narrow, spreading drains. The patterning is most readily apparent on satellite imagery.

The whole area is underlain by peat, which in the vicinity of Highway 72 is over 10 feet thick. The base of this peat is approximately 4000 years old (Ibid., p. 577), and its formation was apparently initiated with the onset of a cooler, moister climate that inhibited the decomposition of vegetation in the poorly drained lowlands.

Scientists at the University of Minnesota are currently studying patterned peatlands. They are trying to understand the origin, the extent, the age, and the vegetational character of the patterning. Several different hypotheses based on geomorphic, biological, and climatic criteria have been presented, but each of these hypotheses is open to criticism. Patterned peatlands in the Hudson Bay lowland owe much of their origin to permafrost. This does not appear to be the case in Minnesota. The most distinctive feature of these patterned mires is the alignment of major landforms with the prevailing land slope. This condition suggests that surface drainage plays an important role in the development of the pattern—that the patterns seem to be associated with the channeling of water (Ibid., p. 591). This hypothesis, however, has not yet been tested, and the study of the patterned peatlands is an ongoing project.

The answers are far from in on the origin of the Red Lake Peatland and its patterning. The problem of its origin must be considered by geologists as well as by botanists and limnologists. The origin of even recent landforms is not a simple problem.

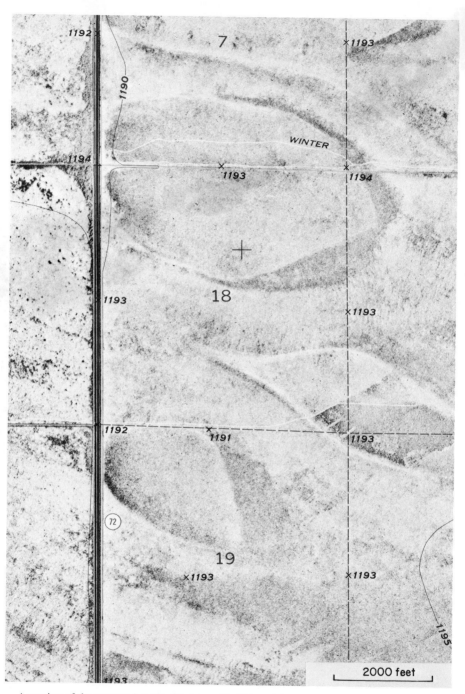

50

A portion of the patterned peatland between Waskish and Baudette.

Typical view of patterned peatland, with tamarack, black spruce, and heath shrubs, between Waskish and Baudette.

Mississippi River and the city of Minneapolis, East Central Minnesota.

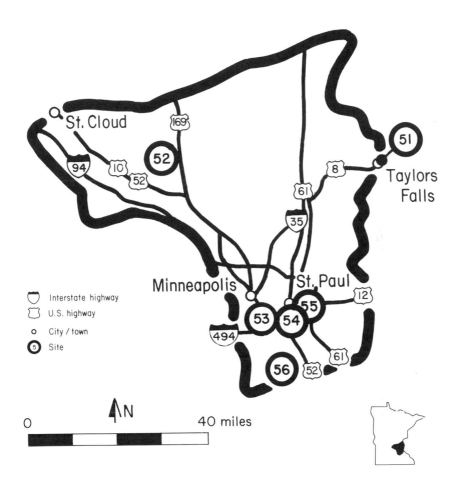

Interstate highway
U.S. highway
City / town
Site

St. Cloud

169

94
10
52
52

St. Paul
Minneapolis
53 54 55
12
494
56 52 61

51
Taylors
Falls

8

61

35

N

0   40 miles

VI East Central Minnesota

Confluence of Mississippi, Minnesota, and St. Croix Rivers

East Central Minnesota is a heavily populated, recently glaciated, small triangular-shaped region at the confluence of the Mississippi, Minnesota, and St. Croix rivers. These rivers have cut through glacial drift and outwash into the flat-lying sedimentary rocks of Paleozoic seas, and in the case of the St. Croix into late Precambrian basalts as well. These rivers are bounded by rocky gorges occasionally more than a mile across and several hundred feet deep. The Twin Cities of Minneapolis and St. Paul are located astride the Mississippi and Minnesota rivers, their populations drawn here by the rivers' hydroelectric power, commerce, and scenery.

This region of East Central Minnesota is defined through the confluence of these three major rivers. It covers the physiographic regions known as the eastern St. Croix moraine and the Anoka sandplain (Wright, *in* Sims and Morey, 1972, p. 564). The region has a young landscape, less than 15,000 years old, of morainal hills and glacial outwash. The region is bounded on the east by the St. Croix River from north of Taylors Falls to near Hastings, on the south and west by the limits of the St. Croix moraine in northern Dakota, Scott, and eastern Hennepin Counties, and on the north by the margin of the Anoka sandplain from near Pine City to St. Cloud.

The St. Croix moraine occupies the eastern and southern portions of this region and is one of the steeper, sharper moraines in Minnesota. It marks the combined limit of the Superior and the Rainy lobes during part of the Wisconsin glaciation. This moraine is lake strewn, often heavily wooded, and composed of thick red and gray drift. It flanks the south side of the Anoka sandplain and extends from St. Paul northeastward into Wisconsin.

The moraine is bordered on the south by the outwash plains of Dakota County. To the west this moraine becomes congruent with the Owatonna and Alexandria moraines. The Anoka sandplain underlies the northern portion of this region. It is a gently undulating area of outwash sands formed as the last glacier melted from East Central Minnesota.

The outwash sands of the Anoka sandplain and the glacial drift of the eastern St. Croix moraine form a thick overburden on both Precambrian and Paleozoic bedrock. Cut into this bedrock is a vast network of river channels, some deeply buried by glacial debris, some presently occupied by rivers.

The oldest rocks exposed in East Central Minnesota are Precambrian basalts, similar to those seen along the North Shore. These dark lavas crop out along the St. Croix River near Taylors Falls in a steep rocky gorge known as the St. Croix Dalles. These basalts and other Precambrian rocks form a basinlike structure surrounding the Twin Cities into which younger and more frequently exposed sediments were laid down as Paleozoic seas inundated this region. These younger rocks—sandstones, shales, and limestones—are seen many places along the St. Croix and Mississippi rivers. Elsewhere in East Central Minnesota, however, they are found only in the subsurface; they are overlain by hundreds of feet of glacial drift and outwash.

East Central Minnesota is thus a very young region, similar in that respect to West Central Minnesota. East Central Minnesota, however, is that portion of Minnesota with a young glaciated landscape dissected by the deep intersecting gorges of the Mississippi, Minnesota, and St. Croix rivers.

The St. Croix River at Interstate State Park, East Central Minnesota.

Dalles of the St. Croix

Interstate Park

COUNTY: **Chisago**
NEAREST TOWN: **Taylors Falls**
OWNERSHIP: **State of Minnesota**
USGS TOPOGRAPHIC MAPS: **St. Croix Dalles, 7½', 1978**

The St. Croix Dalles are a classic location in North American geology. Here at Taylors Falls the St. Croix River plunges into a narrow, rock-bound channel of Precambrian basalt: vertical basalt cliffs rise 150 feet above the river. Overlying that basalt are more than 100 feet of Cambrian siltstones and sandstones. Within the valley are several terraces, the most prominent cut into the basalt and covered with huge potholes. In 1895 the dalles became Minnesota's second state park. Today this park is still a favorite, with its potholes, hiking trails, campgrounds, and excursion boats.

Interstate Park is located along both sides of the St. Croix River at Taylors Falls. The best place to examine the park's geology and to appreciate its natural setting is immediately west of the interstate bridge on the south side of U.S. Highway 8. A short hiking trail begins near the parking lot and information building. This circular path winds among the rocks, beside the potholes, and along the river. The entire hike will take about 30 minutes.

Children particularly enjoy this park—in favorable weather there are rock climbers dressed in their climbing regalia of boots, slings, and helmets; there are canoes and power boats; there are endless games of hide-and-seek along the trails and in the rocks. And the dark, unnatural-looking potholes hold a particular fascination for everyone.

The St. Croix River valley formed in early postglacial time, serving as a glacial meltwater spillway. Later, a large river, the Glacial St. Croix River, flowed through this area. This river drained the waters of glacial lakes in the Lake Superior Basin, cut through the soft Paleozoic sediments and ultimately into an island of Precambrian basalt. The basalt, more resistant than the surrounding sediments, confined the river to a deep, narrow, rock-bound gorge—a dalles. As the river wore through the basalt, it cut rock terraces along its rocky sides and ground potholes into its rocky floor. These potholes range in size from small depressions less than one foot across and one foot deep to huge wells more than 10 feet across and 60 feet deep. More than 80 potholes are found in the small area between the bridge and the boat landing.

Eventually the glaciers moved out of the Great Lakes region and the waters of the Lake Superior basin drained eastward through Lakes Michigan and Huron, the lower Great Lakes, the St. Lawrence River, and into the Atlantic Ocean. The Glacial St. Croix and its tributary rivers, the Kettle and Brule, diminished to their present size and drainage basins.

The basalt flows themselves are of interest. During late Precambrian time a large fracture, or rift, developed across the central United States, from Kansas, through southeastern Minnesota, to Lake Superior and beyond (Chaddock, *in* Sims and Morey, 1972, p. 281). This rift was the site of extensive fissure eruptions, flows of basalt lava, which accumulated to thicknesses greater than 20,000 feet (Sims and Morey, *in* Sims and Morey, 1972, p. 13). Thousands of individual flows make up the entire thickness, and approximately 10 of these flows are exposed at Interstate Park. The individual flows are recognized by their bubble-filled upper surfaces and massive central portions.

Also within this portion of the St. Croix Valley is a segment of one of the most well-exposed and complete sequences of late Cambrian rock anywhere in North America. These rocks, consisting of the Franconia and St. Lawrence formations, tell, though their mineral composition and fossil content, a great deal about the marine environment of this time. This part of the late Cambrian is named the Croixan, from this its type locality.

The area surrounding the St. Croix Dalles is one of major and varied geologic significance. It is doubly blessed by being a region rich in natural beauty and the colorful history of Ojibway Indians, Swedish immigrants, and timber barons. Examine the rocks along the St. Croix River and explore the nearby towns and countryside.

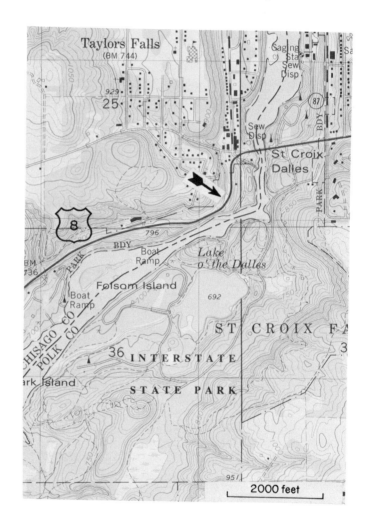

The dalles of the St. Croix at Taylors Falls.

52 Anoka Sandplain

Sand Dunes State Forest

COUNTY: **Sherburne**
NEAREST TOWN: **Orrock**
OWNERSHIP: **State of Minnesota**
USGS TOPOGRAPHIC MAP: **Orrock, 7½',**
1961

The Anoka sandplain covers a large
area between the Mississippi and St.
Croix rivers, north of St. Paul and
south of Milaca, east of St. Cloud and
west of Chisago City. This is the
largest sand and sand dune area within
Minnesota. The geologic consensus is
that this unstable sand country was
formed as a series of coalescing outwash plains during the retreat of the last
glacier as its meltwaters first found
their way into the St. Croix River and
then into the Mississippi River (Wright,
in Sims and Morey, 1972, p. 570).
Sand dunes were later superimposed on
this plain by local wind action. During
the drought years of the 1930s drifting
sands, dunes, and sand storms threat-
ened the local communities, and a program of reforestation was begun. Today
the vast proportion of this area has been
reforested and the sand stabilized.
However, due to its droughty soils, this
region is still agriculturally poor, and
the forest and grassland vegetation is
sparse compared with other regions of
Minnesota.

Sand Dunes State Forest occupies
10,800 acres in the northeastern portion
of the Anoka sandplain. The forest is
approximately 15 miles north of
Minneapolis–St. Paul. The entrance to
the forest is on the south side of County
Road 4, four miles east of Orrock, six
miles west of Zimmerman. Turn south
onto the entrance road and drive to the
lake and campground. Park there below
the lookout tower. Climb to the top of
the lookout tower for an excellent view
of the surrounding countryside.

Most of the Anoka sandplain is almost
flat, with many sections in which the
local relief is less than 10 feet. There
are broad, level, abandoned fields punc-
tuated by slightly higher or lower
ground of oak savannah, aspen grove,
and marsh. The sandplain, however, is
not entirely featureless. There are
regions of upland which represent areas
of glacial till not completely buried by
the outwash sands. There are patches of
sand dunes formed by southwesterly
winds after the plain was abandoned by
the outwash streams. There are
numerous streams and marshes resulting
from the melting of ice blocks, and
there are some long, southwest-trending
troughs representing buried valleys
(Ibid.).

This broad sandplain is not unlike
other sand or outwash plains in Minnesota (see Site #43); however it is
larger than the others, and it is one of
the very few where sand dunes are
prominent. Sand dunes exist on portions
of the Brainerd outwash plain. They
also exist on Minnesota Point near
Duluth and on the Mississippi River terraces between Weaver and Kellogg. The
Anoka sandplain, as the largest area of
dunes within Minnesota, has consequently received the greatest effort
toward dune stabilization.

The sparse native vegetation of prairie
grass, oak savannah, and thin deciduous
forest has been replaced by thickly
planted jack and red pine. These plant-
ings have successfully stabilized the
dunes and are now becoming a small
economic resource for the state.

It is interesting to note that Oregon
has successfully stabilized its coastal
dunes through the introduction of Euro-
pean beach grass. Their program has
been so effective, in fact, that people
are now concerned that they will lose
their active dunes—a major recreational
resource of that state. Minnesota's
dunes, however, are not a primary
recreational attraction for the state, and
eliminating the potential of devastating
sand storms is far more important.

Typical view of the Anoka sandplain showing low hills and shallow marshes.

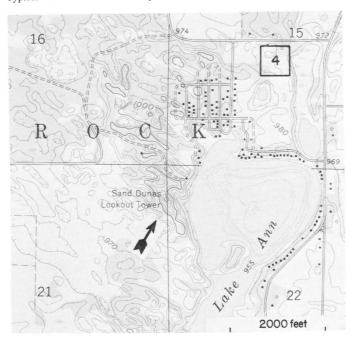

A portion of Sand Dunes State Forest near Orrock.

53 Confluence of the Mississippi and Minnesota Rivers

Fort Snelling, Minneapolis

COUNTY: **Hennepin**
NEAREST TOWN: **Minneapolis**
OWNERSHIP: **U.S. Government**
USGS TOPOGRAPHIC MAP: **St. Paul West, 7½', 1967**

Minnesota's largest rivers, the Mississippi and Minnesota, join together in the Twin Cities of Minneapolis and St. Paul. Above their confluence the Mississippi flows in a steep, narrow gorge; the Minnesota flows in a much broader, less steep-sided valley. The history of these rivers, their valleys, and their confluence is the story of erosion and deposition, of changing water levels, and of the migration of waterfalls. It is also the story of meticulous and accurate geologic observation and deduction. These rivers join below old Fort Snelling, an important site in Minnesota territorial history.

Fort Snelling is located on a rock terrace at the west end of the Mendota Bridge near the junction of Minnesota highways 55 and 5. From either highway follow the signs to the fort. Park north of the fort, then walk to its northeast corner. Look downstream along the Mississippi. A better vantage point for the two rivers is from the semicircular battery within the fort. A second observation point for the Mississippi and Minnesota rivers is at the southwest end of Cherokee Heights Park. This park is located on the south side of the Mississippi along Minnesota Highway 13, approximately five miles east of the Mendota Bridge. Look upstream from the park toward the confluence of the two rivers and note the

broad valley and the bordering terraces. Also note the moraine at Highland Park and Mendota Heights.

The Mississippi River before and during glacial times cut many rock channels through the Twin Cities. Most of these are now deeply buried by glacial till and outwash (see Site #55). The river cut its present channel after final ice retreat, as the glacial meltwaters found their way southward through the hilly St. Croix moraine. During the channel-cutting process and in response to changing water volume and local base level, terraces formed along the valley's sides. One particularly evident terrace is at 810 feet—this is the terrace on which is built Fort Snelling and numerous apartments and fuel storage tanks.

While the Mississippi River was finding a path through the St. Croix moraine, Glacial Lake Agassiz was forming in Northwestern Minnesota (see Introduction to Region V). Glacial River Warren, the large outlet stream for that lake, flowed across central Minnesota and joined the far smaller Mississippi River near Fort Snelling. Together both rivers flowed east and south through St. Paul.

Immediately downstream from St. Paul the river cut across a buried valley, quickly removed the fill from that valley, and formed a large waterfall known as the River Warren Falls. This waterfall, as much as 300 feet high and one mile across, slowly migrated upstream to Fort Snelling (INQUA, 1965, p. 48). From this point the falls split and continued separate migrations up Glacial River Warren and up the Mississippi River. Two miles upstream from Fort Snelling (in Bloomington), Glacial River Warren intersected another buried channel and River Warren Falls was extinguished. Meanwhile, the other branch of this large falls, now known as St. Anthony Falls, retreated up the Mississippi. Today this latter falls is still in existence eight miles above Fort Snelling.

Eventually, as the ice sheet retreated,

Glacial Lake Agassiz emptied to the north: the high-volume, low-load Glacial River Warren became the low-volume, high-load Minnesota River. The Minnesota River valley began to fill with sediments (Site #29). Today the present floodplain of both rivers is underlain by 80 feet of alluvial material near Fort Snelling and 275 feet of alluvial material at South St. Paul (Wright, *in* Sims and Morey, 1972, p. 537).

The rate of erosion, or retreat, of River Warren Falls and St. Anthony Falls has been used to estimate the length of postglacial time. In 1888, N. H. Winchell, state geologist and director, Geological and Natural History Survey, noted the position of St. Anthony Falls at the time it was discovered by Father Hennepin in 1680 and seven times during the next 200 years. He calculated the average rate of

retreat at 5.08 feet per year, for a total of 8315 years for the falls to retreat eight miles from Fort Snelling (INQUA, 1965, p. 48). In 1916, F. W. Sardeson, saying that several important factors were not constant—the thickness of the capping limestone, the height of the falls, and the volume of water—recalculated and got 12,000 years as the time of retreat from Fort Snelling and 8000 years since the end of Glacial River Warren.

Today, highly consistent radiocarbon dates indicate that Glacial River Warren was in existence from 11,700 to 9200 years ago. Warren Falls had thus started in St. Paul about 11,700 years ago and had migrated the 10 miles to its extinction in Bloomington by 9200 years ago. The falls must therefore have passed Fort Snelling by 10,300 years ago. Winchell's figure of 8315 years for St. Anthony Falls to retreat from Fort

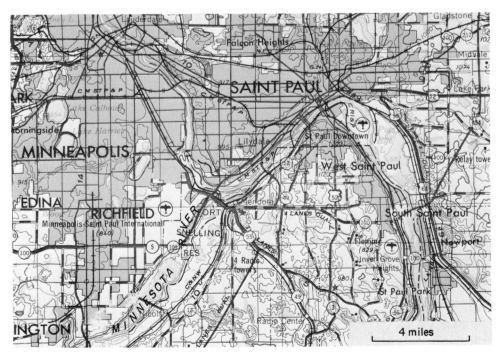

The course of the Mississippi and Minnesota rivers in Minneapolis–St. Paul, from the USGS St. Paul 1:250,000, 1953 (limited revision 1963).

Snelling is thus only about 20% too short. Sardeson's figure of 12,000 years to retreat from Fort Snelling is 16% too long (Ibid., pp. 49 and 51).

Recent evaluation of the radiocarbon time scale indicates that the 9200 year carbon date equals about 10,000 years and that this figure is midway between Winchell's and Sardeson's estimates (Wright, *in* Sims and Morey, 1972, p. 539). This is a remarkable confirmation that careful geologic observation and deduction of erosional rates rival in their accuracy the geochemical method of radiocarbon dating.

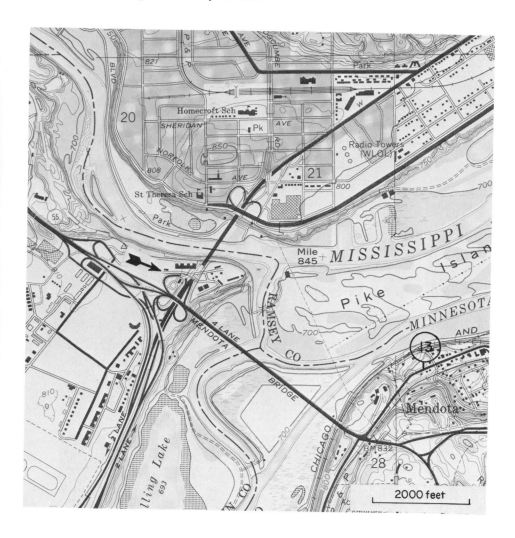

Mississippi River at its confluence with the Minnesota River, from Fort Snelling.

54 St. Peter Sandstone

West St. Paul

COUNTY: **Ramsey**
NEAREST TOWN: **West St. Paul**
OWNERSHIP: **Ramsey County**
USGS TOPOGRAPHIC MAP: **St. Paul East, 7½', 1967**

The St. Peter Sandstone is a 100-foot-thick layer of generally white, uniformly medium-grained quartz sandstone. This rock is unusual because of its uniform grain size, single mineral composition, and great areal extent. This is one of the world's purest quartz sandstones and covers a large area of the central United States, cropping out in Southeastern and East Central Minnesota, as well as portions of Wisconsin, Illinois, Indiana, Ohio, Iowa, Missouri, Kansas, Oklahoma, Arkansas, and Kentucky. The St. Peter Sandstone represents the marginal deposits of an Ordovician sea and has been used to demonstrate that rocks of similar composition and texture are formed in the same environment rather than at the same time. The sandstone may be seen along the Mississippi River downstream from the Washington Avenue Bridge. It also forms the large white cliffs below Fort Snelling and receives its name from that location on the St. Peter, now Minnesota, River. The rock is most accessible at the old Twin Cities Brickyard, now a Ramsey County park.

The old brickyard is located on the south side of the Mississippi River near the town of Lilydale. It is immediately south of and below Cherokee Heights Park. From downtown St. Paul drive southward across the Wabasha Street Bridge. Then turn right onto Water Street. Follow Water Street southwest under the High Bridge and along the river. The road forks at 1.2 miles. Take the left-hand fork—do not cross under the railroad trestle—and proceed 0.3 mile to the park.

The St. Peter Sandstone crops out all along Water Street, where it is full of natural caves formed in postglacial times by a rapidly dropping water table. These caves, like other caves throughout the Twin Cities, have been enlarged and used for mushroom culture, cheese storage, beer storage, boat storage, storm sewers, and even a ballroom. Caves within the park were once used as brick kilns.

The St. Peter Sandstone, because of its great areal extent, exceedingly uniform texture, and pure mineralogy, is easily recognized in the field and has been the subject of many geologic studies. The rock is 99% pure quartz sand and generally a striking white, but it is occasionally iron-stained to orange, yellow, or brown. The rock at the brickyard is a dirty off-white due to soil wash and soot. The rock is loosely cemented, but, as here, often has a thin, hard surface coating of calcite. Once this calcite coating is broken, the rock falls into a million pieces of sand.

The St. Peter Sandstone, worked and reworked from earlier Cambrian sandstones, was deposited along the edge of an Ordovician sea when, during middle Ordovician times, a sea encroached northward over North America. The sand was deposited both on the beach and in shallow water. Finer sediments, silts, clays, and carbonates were deposited farther out to sea. As the sea moved northward, it kept depositing sand along its shores and finer sediments in deeper water. Hence, the St. Peter Sandstone of Missouri is older than the St. Peter Sandstone of Minnesota.

Geologists once believed that rocks of similar composition had all been formed at the same time. The St. Peter Sandstone, along with many other rock units, has shown this belief to be untrue. Rocks of similar composition are formed in similar environments, not necessarily at the same time. Rocks deposited on beaches are different than those deposited in deep water; rocks laid down on land are different from those laid down in water; igneous rocks cooled deep within the earth are different from those which have cooled on the earth's surface. Sands deposited along the shore of an Ordovician sea could look like those deposited along a modern sea, but they could not look like those deposited alongside a large river.

(Site #54)

The St. Peter Sandstone has had a variety of uses. It is used for sandblasting and filtration. It is also a beautiful sandbox sand, although being of such small and uniform grain size, it seeps into every pocket and cuff, into ears, hair, and shoes. Watch for this geologically world-renowned sandstone along the river gorges and freeway cuts within the Twin Cities, and watch for it throughout Southeastern Minnesota, along the mesas and highways near Stanton and Cannon Falls, and near the Zumbro River in Rochester.

Boys at the entrance to a cave in St. Peter Sandstone, at the old Twin Cities Brickyard.

55 Buried River Valleys

Mounds Park, St. Paul

COUNTY: **Ramsey**
NEAREST TOWN: **St. Paul**
OWNERSHIP: **City of St. Paul**
USGS TOPOGRAPHIC MAP: **St. Paul East, 7½', 1967**

The Twin Cities of Minneapolis and St. Paul are underlain by a vast network of buried river valleys. These valleys, formed during preglacial and glacial times, are filled now with several hundred feet of glacial drift and outwash. These channels are often larger but otherwise not very different from those of the present-day Mississippi and Minnesota rivers. They were cut by these rivers before they reached their present courses. These buried channels are marked today, if at all, by occasional strings of lakes or by subdued valleys. Nowhere may they be seen directly. Mounds Park is an excellent vantage point for the present Mississippi channel. From the park may also be seen traces of two buried channels.

Mounds Park is located in St. Paul approximately 1.5 miles east of downtown. It is located on the top of the south-facing Mississippi River bluff. Take Interstate Highway 94 to Mounds Boulevard. Follow Mounds Boulevard for approximately 0.5 mile to Mounds Park. Stop near the large Indian mounds and walk westward beyond the big tower. Look both up and down the present Misssissippi River. Immediately northwest of Mounds Park, just east of downtown St. Paul, is a lowland occupied by railroad tracks; this lowland is the trace of a buried valley. This particular valley runs north-northeast up through Lakes McCarron, Josephine, and Johanna. A second buried valley joins the present Mississippi River valley approximately 0.5 mile east of Mounds Park. This second valley runs north under Phalen, Round, Keller, Gervais, Kohlman, Willow, Gene, and eventually Goose, White Bear, and Birch lakes. The westward branch of this channel cuts northwestward through Little Canada and underneath Savage, Vadnais, Grass, and Snail lakes (Payne, 1965, map).

In preglacial and glacial times the Mississippi River, as today, flowed through the Twin Cities. During glacial times it served as a meltwater passageway, flowing through the Twin Cities and cutting deep bedrock valleys. With each ice advance preexisting channels were buried, filled with glacial debris. With the melting of the ice new rivers and new valleys were formed. Eventually a whole network of valleys developed. Many of these valleys, now buried, were more than 300 feet deep and many miles in length.

The Mississippi River established its modern course in postglacial time, as meltwater from the Wisconsin ice broke through the St. Croix moraine. At Mounds Park the present valley is 227 feet deep and 1.5 miles across. The bedrock floor of the valley, however, is another 137 feet deeper (Ibid.).

Buried valleys are found not only in St. Paul but also in Minneapolis and elsewhere throughout Minnesota. In Minneapolis, Wirth Lake, Cedar Lake, Lake of the Isles, Lake Calhoun, and Lake Harriet all occupy the course of a buried valley. Another buried valley is marked by Lakes Hiawatha and Nokomis. Lakes Itasca, Alcon, and Mary occupy a buried valley in Itasca State Park (see Site #38). The north-south strings of lakes running through Alexandria and through northwestern and central Martin County have also formed within buried bedrock valleys. Other buried valleys will be found as geologists continue their subsurface mapping.

Mississippi River and the city of St. Paul from Mounds Park.

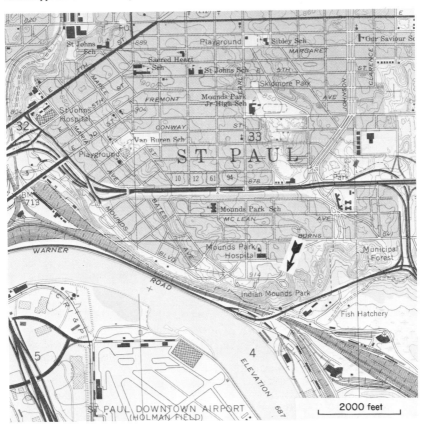

(Site #55)

56 Kirchner Marsh

Dakota County

COUNTY: **Dakota**
NEAREST TOWN: **Inver Grove Heights**
OWNERSHIP: **Private—view from public roadway**
USGS TOPOGRAPHIC MAP: **Inver Grove Heights, 7½', 1967**

Within Kirchner Marsh is a detailed record of Minnesota's postglacial vegetation and climate. This marsh is a typical ice-block depression, a water-filled low spot in the rolling morainal country south of St. Paul. It is little different from other marshes within Minnesota—it is extraordinary only in the fact that its sediments have been so thoroughly studied. Like most other Minnesota lakes and marshes, it has slowly become sediment filled during the past 12,000 or so years. These sediments contain pollen, seeds, and various invertebrates and give a most unusual and complete stratigraphic record of postglacial events.

Kirchner Marsh is located approximately 12 miles south of St. Paul and approximately two miles north of Rosemount. The cattail-covered marsh is found along the west side of Minnesota Highway 3 in the northeast quarter of section 17, Rosemount Township. Park carefully off the roadway and look westward across the marsh.

The sediments of Kirchner Marsh have been carefully studied by geologists, botanists, and limnologists at the University of Minnesota. Similar to other studies within the Midwest and throughout the world, these studies have shown that particular regions have undergone vegetational, and hence climatic, change throughout postglacial time. The vegetation has been different for different regions of the world, but the climatic trends indicated by this vegetation are worldwide.

Kirchner Marsh formed approximately 12,700 years ago as an ice-block depression within the St. Croix moraine (Wright, 1970, glacial geology notes). Once this depression had formed, it rapidly gathered sediment from the nearby, unvegetated and unstable hillsides. Soon forest grew over the barren deglaciated ground, and marsh plants began to infringe on the lake-filled depression. Pollen and seeds from these plants blew and fell into the lake, sank to the bottom, and became trapped in the lake bottom sediments. Cores take from these sediments show changes over time in the types and relative abundances of pollen, seeds, and invertebrates. Careful study of the sediments reveals the vegetational history of the area and gives clues to the changing climate.

Study of the sediments of Kirchner Marsh and other Minnesota marshes has shown that southern Minnesota supported a spruce forest until around 12,000 years ago, when north central Minnesota supported tundra vegetation and northern Minnesota was still under glacial ice. By approximately 11,500 years ago ice had finally left the state, and the spruce forest had spread northward across Minnesota. In subsequent years, as the climate became warmer and drier, the spruce forests in southern Minnesota were rapidly replaced by birch, alder, pine, oak, and prairie. By 7000 years ago the warming and drying trend had reached a maximum and the prairie-forest border in Minnesota was approximately 75 miles northeast of its present position (refer to accompanying diagram). The region surrounding Kirchner Marsh was located on the prairie-forest boundary in a region of oak savannah. Between 7000 years ago and the present there has been a reversal of this warming and drying trend; gradually prairie has been invaded by forest, and the coniferous forests of the north advanced into the deciduous forest farther south (Ibid.).

Lake sediments have recorded major changes in environmental conditions within the past 100 years. Increased sedimentation rates have resulted from the clearing of land for agriculture. A sudden and marked increase in the pollen of particular plants indicates the introduction and abundance of certain crops and agricultural weeds. Greater organic accumulation has resulted from greater vegetative production. This vegetative production has in turn resulted from increased nutrient levels due to surface runoff of fertilizer and animal waste and underground seepage of human waste. Sediments within certain lakes and marshes show sudden and rapid accumulations of particular heavy metals, the result of man's industrial expansion.

The rise and demise of the spruce forest, oak savannah, and prairie are all recorded within the lake sediments, as is the rise of agriculture and industry. Will agriculture's and industry's demise someday be marked within those sediments? Many Minnesota lakes and marshes have been faithfully documenting environmental conditions for 12,000 years. What will they record in the coming 12,000 years?

Sediments and rocks record history without bias; they document human history and geologic history, pollution and mountain building. Their tale is continuously open to geologic investigation. Sediments and sedimentary rocks, formed in lakes and marshes, oceans and swamps, record whatever falls into them and can be preserved. Igneous and metamorphic rocks tell of eruptions and intrusions, heat and pressure. Sediments and rocks exist everywhere underfoot in Minnesota, a faithful record of the past and ultimately a faithful record of the future.

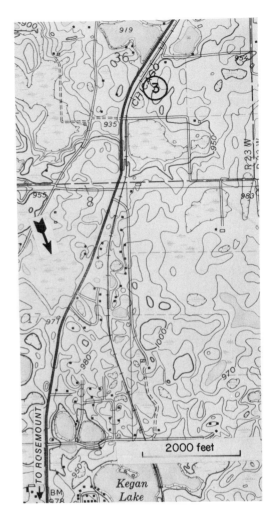

Kirchner Marsh, near Rosemount.

Maplewood State Park (35)

Inspiration Peak (34)

CONIFER - HARDWOOD FOREST

HARDWOOD FOREST

Kirchner Marsh (56)

PRAIRIE

Vegetation of Minnesota circa 1850

Cited References

American Geological Institute. *Dictionary of Geological Terms*. Garden City: Anchor Press/Doubleday, 1976.

Atwood, Wallace W. *The Physiographic Provinces of North America*. Boston: Ginn & Co., 1940.

Austin, George S. "Paleozoic Stratigraphic Nomenclature for Southeastern Minnesota." Minneapolis: Minnesota Geologic Survey, 1969.

Carlson, George. Hydrologist, USGS Hydrological Survey, Water Division, St. Paul, Minnesota.

Craddock, Campbell, *in* Sims and Morey, 1972. "Regional Geologic Setting," pp. 281–91.

Davidson, Donald M., Jr., *in* Sims and Morey, 1972. "Eastern Part of Duluth Complex," pp. 354–60.

Flint, Richard Foster. *Glacial and Pleistocene Geology*. New York: John Wiley and Sons, Inc., 1957.

Glaser, Paul H.; Wheeler, Gerald; Gorham, Eville; and Wright, H. E., Jr. "The Patterned Mires of the Red Lake Peatland, Northern Minnesota: Vegetation, Water Chemistry and Landforms." *Journal of Ecology*, Vol. 69., pp. 575–99, 1981.

Goldich, S. S., *in* Sims and Morey, 1972. "Geochronology in Minnesota," pp. 27–37.

Grant, J. A.; Himmelberg, G. R.; and Goldich, S. S. *Field Trip Guidebook for the Precambrian Migmatitic Terrane of the Minnesota River Valley*. Minneapolis: Minnesota Geological Survey, 1972.

Grout, F. F.; Sharp, R. P.; and Schwartz, G. M. *The Geology of Cook County, Minnesota*. Minneapolis: University of Minnesota Press, 1959.

Hogberg, R. K., and Matsch, C. L. "A Teacher's Guide for Geologic Field Investigation in Central Minnesota." *in* W. Phinney, editor, *A Teacher's Guide for Geologic Field Investigations in Minnesota*. Minnesota Department of Education, Minnesota Geological Survey, [1967].

International Association for Quaternary Research (INQUA), VIIth Congress. "Guidebook for Field Conference C: Upper Mississippi Valley." 1965.

Iron Ranges Resources and Rehabiliation Board. "Rochleau Group, Virginia, Minnesota." undated.

Kresbach, Ted. Cold Spring Granite Company, Cold Spring, Minnesota.

Matsch, C. L.; Tipton, M. J.; Steece, F. J.; Rutford, R. H.; and Parham, W. E. *Field Trip Guidebook for Geomorphology and Quaternary Stratigraphy of Western Minnesota and Eastern South Dakota*. Minneapolis: Minnesota Geological Survey, 1972.

Matsch, C. L., and Wright, H. E., Jr. "The Southern Outlet of Lake Agassiz" *in* W. J. Mayer-Oakes, editor, "Life, Land and Water," Conference on environmental studies of the Glacial Lake Agassiz region. Winnipeg: University of Manitoba Press, 1966.

Morey, G. B. Geologic Map of Minnesota: Bedrock Geology. St Paul: Minnesota Geological Survey.

Oberdorfer, Dan. "Sinkholes Funneling Litter into Water Supply," *The Minneapolis Tribune*, Nov. 19, 1981, pp. 3B, 10B.

Ojakangas, R. W., and Morey, G. B. *Field Trip Guidebook for Lower Precambrian Volcanic-Sedimentary Rocks of the Vermilion District, Minnesota*. Minneapolis: Minnesota Geological Survey, 1972.

Payne, C. Marshall. *Bedrock Geologic Map of Minneapolis, St. Paul, and Vicinity*. Minneapolis: Minnesota Geological Survey, 1965.

Phinney, William, *in* Sims and Morey, 1972. "Duluth Complex: History and Nomenclature," pp. 333–34.

Schwartz, G. M. "Geology of Gooseberry State Park," in *The Conservation Volunteer*, Vol. XI, pp. 18–19, Jan–Feb. 1948.

Schwartz, George, and Thiel, George. *Minnesota's Rocks and Waters: A Geological Story*. Minneapolis: University of Minnesota Press, 1954.

Searle, R. Newell, and Heitlinger, Mark E. *Prairies, Woods and Islands: A Guide to the Minnesota Preserves of The Nature Conservancy*. The Nature Conservancy, 1980.

Seehausen, John. Mayor of Morton, Minnesota.

Sims, P. K., *in* Sims and Morey, 1972. "Bonded Iron-Formations in Vermillion District," pp. 79–81.

Sims, P. K., *in* Sims and Morey, 1972. "Metavolcanic and Associated Synvolcanic Rocks in the Vermilion District," pp. 63–75.

Sims, P. K., *in* Sims and Morey, 1972. "Northern Minnesota, General Geologic Features," pp. 41–48.

Sims, P. K., and Morey, G. B., editors. *Geology of Minnesota: A Centennial Volume*. Minneapolis: Minnesota Geological Survey, 1972.

Sims, P. K., and Morey, G. B., *in* Sims and Morey, 1972. "Resumé of Geology of Minnesota," pp. 3–20.

Sims, P. K., and Viswanathan, J., *in* Sims and Morey, 1972. "Giants Range Batholith," pp. 120–39.

Sloan, R. E., and Weiss, M. P., *in* Schwartz, G. M., ed. "Lower Paleozoic of the Upper Mississippi Valley: Field Trip #2." Geological Society of America, 1956.

Taylor, Richard B. *Bedrock Geology of Duluth and Vicinity, St. Louis County, Minnesota*. Minneapolis: University of Minnesota Press, 1963.

Taylor, Richard B. *Geology of the Duluth Gabbro Complex near Duluth, Minnesota*. Minneapolis: University of Minnesota Press, 1964.

Thiel, George A. *The Geology and Underground Waters of Southern Minnesota*. Minneapolis, The University of Minnesota Press, 1944.

Weiblen, Paul W., and Morey, G. B. "A Summary of the Stratigraphy, Petrology, and Structure of the Duluth Complex." *American Journal of Science*, Vol. 280-A, pp. 88–133, 1980.

Windley, Brian F. *The Evolving Continents*. Chichester: John Wiley and Sons, 1977.

Wright, H. E., Jr., Director of the Limnological Research Center and Regents Professor of Geology, Department of Geology and Geophysics. University of Minnesota, Minneapolis.

Wright, H. E., Jr., *in* Sims and Morey, 1972. "Physiography of Minnesota." pp. 561–78.

Wright, H. E., Jr., *in* Sims and Morey, 1972. "Quaternary History of Minnesota," pp. 515–47.

Wright, H. E., Jr., Glacial Geology Notes, autumn 1970. University of Minnesota, Minneapolis.

Zumberge, James H. *The Lakes of Minnesota: Their Origin and Classification*. Minneapolis: The University of Minnesota Press, 1952.

216   *Cited References*

Suggested Readings

*Alexander, E. Calvin, Jr., editor. *An Introduction to Caves of Minnesota, Iowa, and Wisconsin: Guidebook for the 1980 National Speleological Society Convention*. The National Speleological Society, 1980. This book presents a synopsis, including line diagrams, of 38 commercial and wild caves.

*Hogberg, R. K.; Sloan, R. E.; and Tufford, Sarah. "Guide to Fossil Collecting in Minnesota." Minneapolis: The Minnesota Geological Survey, 1967. This pamphlet, undergoing revision, is easy to read and liberally illustrated.

**Moyle, John B.; Moyle, Evelyn W. *Northland Wild Flowers: A Guide for the Minnesota Region*. Minneapolis: University of Minnesota Press, 1977. *Northland Wild Flowers* is an excellent and colorful guide to 300 Minnesota wild flowers. Each plant is discussed as to its characteristics and its pattern of occurrence.

Ojakangas, Richard W.; Matsch, Charles L. *Minnesota Geology*. Minneapolis: University of Minnesota Press, 1982. A newly published, profusely illustrated text on Minnesota geology, presented as an updated companion to *Minnesota's Rocks and Waters*.

**Rosendahl, Carl O. *Trees and Shrubs of the Upper Midwest*. Minneapolis: University of Minnesota Press, 1955. This book is recommended, although technical in nature, as the authority on midwestern trees and shrubs. Perhaps of more interest to the casual reader would be any one of the innumerable guide books put out by the Golden Press in New York, the Houghton Mifflin Company in Boston, and other sources.

Searle, R. Newell; Heitlinger, Mark E. *Prairies, Woods, and Islands: A Guide to the Minnesota Preserves of The Nature Conservancy*. The Nature Conservancy, 1980. This book, available through The Nature Conservancy, Minnesota Chapter (328 East Hennepin Avenue, Minneapolis, Minnesota 55414), discusses each Minnesota preserve—its location, its geographic, botanic, and zoologic features.

**Schwartz, George M.; Thiel, George A. *Minnesota's Rocks and Waters: A Geological Story*. Minneapolis: The University of Minnesota Press, 1954. This highly readable and well-illustrated book has long been the standard by which other Minnesota geology books have been judged.

*Schwartz, George M.; Thiel, George A. "Guide to the Minerals and Rocks of Minnesota." Minneapolis: Department of Geology and Minnesota Geological Survey, University of Minnesota, 1960. This short guide is an excellent and thorough introduction to the characteristics and occurrence of both Minnesota's common and uncommon minerals and rocks.

**Shelton, John S. *Geology Illustrated*. San Francisco and London: W. H. Freeman and

*Available from the Minnesota Geological Survey, 2610 University Avenue, St. Paul, Minnesota 55114.
**Available through your local library.

Company, 1965. This introductory geology text is noteworthy for its almost 400 photographs of landscapes and rocks.

***Sims, P. K.; Morey, G. B., editors. *Geology of Minnesota: A Centennial Volume*. St. Paul: Minnesota Geological Survey, 1972. This very large and technical book has two chapters of interest to the general reader: Chapter I, "Resumé of Geology of Minnesota" by P. K. Sims and G. B. Morey, with a portion of Chapter VII, entitled "Physiography of Minnesota," by H. E. Wright, Jr.

**Waters, Thomas F. *The Streams and Rivers of Minnesota*. Minneapolis: The University of Minnesota Press, 1977. This book discusses the major watersheds of Minnesota, describing the physical, biological, and historical aspects of the rivers and streams of that region. The book should be of interest to canoeists, fishermen, ecologists, and other outdoor-oriented people.

Glossary

ABRADE—to wear away or erode.

ACTINOLITE—an iron-rich amphibole.

AGATE—a brightly colored, banded rock composed of silicon dioxide.

AGGLOMERATE—a volcanic rock composed predominantly of rounded rock fragments.

ALLUVIAL—a general term pertaining to sediments deposited by lakes and streams.

ALLUVIUM—unconsolidated rock materials which have been transported by water.

AMPHIBOLE—an often dark-colored group of silicate minerals.

AMPHIBOLITE—a crystalline rock consisting mainly of amphibole and plagioclase feldspar.

AMYGDULE—a gas cavity within an igneous rock which has been filled with such secondary minerals as zeolite, calcite, or quartz.

ANORTHOSITE—an intrusive igneous rock composed almost entirely of plagioclase feldspar.

AQUIFER—a water-bearing rock layer.

AUGITE—a generally dark-colored silicate mineral, (Ca,Na) (Mg,Fe,Al) $(Si,-Al)_2O_6$.

BASALT—a dark-colored, fine-grained igneous rock.

BATHOLITH—an extremely large stock or shield-shaped mass of igneous rock.

BED—the smallest division of layered rock marked by planes above and below.

BEDROCK—any solid rock exposed at the surface of the earth or overlain by unconsolidated, loose, rock material.

BENTONITE—an altered volcanic rock.

BIOTITE—a dark-colored mica.

BOREAL—northern.

BRECCIA—a rock made up of angular fragments of other rocks.

CALCAREOUS—containing calcium carbonate.

CARBONATE—a compound containing the radical CO_3^{+2}. Calcium carbonate, $CaCO_3$, is the major component of limestone.

CEMENT—any chemically precipitated material holding together the particles in clastic rocks.

CHERT—a variety of quartz.

CHLORITE—a generally green-colored metamorphic mineral.

CLASTIC—composed of rock fragments.

COMPLEX—an assemblage of rocks of any age or origin which have been intricately mixed together.

CRYSTALLINE—composed of crystals.

DEFORMATION—any change in rock form or volume, normally produced by folding or faulting.

DENDRITIC—branchlike.

DIABASE—an intrusive, generally dark-colored igneous rock of basaltic composition.

*These definitions pertain only to the word use in this text; for further information check the AGI *Dictionary of Geological Terms*, American Geological Institute, 1976.

DIFFERENTIAL EROSION—the more rapid erosion in one portion of the landscape than another.

DIFFERENTIATION—the process by which a change in mineral composition occurs within a particular rock body. This is often accomplished through gravitational separation.

DIKE—a tabular body of igneous rock that cuts across the structure of adjacent rocks.

DIORITE—an intrusive igneous rock, usually medium grained and consisting mostly of dark minerals. Small amounts of quartz and light-colored feldspar may be present.

DIP-SLIP FAULT—a fault with primary movement parallel to the dip of the fault.

DOLOMITE—a common rock-forming mineral, $(Ca,Mg)CaCO_3$.

DRIFT, GLACIAL DRIFT—any rock material, sorted or unsorted, deposited as a result of glaciation.

DRUMLIN—an elongate hill composed of glacial drift.

EMPLACEMENT—the movement to a particular position, used in reference to intrusive rocks.

EPIDOTE—a silicate mineral common in metamorphic rocks and generally greenish in color.

ERRATIC—a glacially transported rock.

ESKER—an elongate, often sinuous ridge composed of stratified sands and gravels. Eskers probably mark the channels of subglacial streams.

EXTRUSIVE—igneous rocks which cooled on the surface of the earth.

FAULT—a plane along which rocks have broken and moved.

FELDSPAR—a group of common rock-forming minerals. These are silicate minerals and are the most widespread of any mineral group; they comprise 60% of the earth's crust.

FELSITE—a light-colored igneous rock.

FERRIC—containing iron (valence +3).

FERROUS—containing iron (valence +2).

FLOODPLAIN—the portion of a river valley adjacent to the river channel. It is underlain by sediments deposited by the river and covered with water when the river overflows its banks during floods.

FLOWSTONE—a deposit of calcium carbonate which accumulates when water trickles into rock cavities. It is often found in caves.

FOLD—any bend in rock structure.

FORMATION—a rock unit which is mappable, of distinct composition, and easily recognized in the field.

FOSSIL—any remains or trace of ancient life.

GABBRO—a dark-colored, coarse-grained intrusive igneous rock.

GEOMORPHIC—pertaining to landforms.

GLACIER—a moving mass of ice.

GLAUCONITE—"greensand," an iron potassium silicate occurring in Paleozoic sedimentary rocks of marine origin.

GNEISS—a banded metamorphic rock.

GRANITE—a common, coarse-grained intrusive igneous rock. Granite consists primarily of light-colored minerals, alkali feldspar and quartz, but also contains smaller amounts of dark minerals, generally biotite, hornblende, and pyroxene.

GRAPTOLITE—an extinct colonial organism generally considered to be a primitive chordate.

GRAVITY AND FLOW SEPARATION—the separation of heavier and larger crystals by weight and motion.

GREENSTONE—an altered mafic volcanic rock which owes its color to the presence of chlorite, hornblende, and epidote.

HORNBLENDE—a dark-colored silicate mineral of the amphibole group.

ICE-BLOCK LAKE—a lake formed by the melting of a buried ice-block.

ICE-MARGIN LAKE—a lake formed at the margin of a glacier.

ICE RAMPART—an unstratified ridge of unconsolidated materials found along lake shores and formed by ice push and ice shove.

IGNEOUS ROCK—any rock formed by the cooling of molten rock material, either within or upon the earth.

INTRUSION—any body of igneous rock that invades another older rock.

INTRUSIVE—igneous rocks formed below the earth's surface.

IRON-FORMATION—a chemically deposited sedimentary rock containing at least 15% iron and commonly containing chert.

JASPILITE—a rock consisting of alternating bands of red jasper, a variety of quartz, and iron oxides.

KAME—a conical hill of stratified sand and gravel deposited in contact with glacial ice.

KARST—a type of topography formed by the dissolution of limestone, dolomite, and gypsum. It is characterized by sinkholes, caves, and underground drainage.

KNOB AND KETTLE—a morainal topography of irregular hills and holes.

LABRADORITE—a type of plagioclase feldspar with nearly equal proportions of calcium and sodium.

LACUSTRINE—lake deposited.

LANDFORM—one of the features that make up the surface of the earth, includes such large broad features as plains and plateaus and also more irregular, smaller features such as hills and valleys.

LIMESTONE—a sedimentary rock consisting primarily of calcium carbonate.

LIMNOLOGIST—a person who studies lakes.

LIMONITE—a brown-to-yellow mineral or rock containing hydrous iron oxides.

LITHOLOGIC—pertaining to rocks.

LOESS—wind-deposited silt.

LOPOLITH—basin-shaped body of intrusive igneous rock.

MAFIC—''dark minerals'' found in igneous rock. A mafic rock is composed dominantly of magnesium rock-forming silicates. *Mafic* is used in contrast to *felsic*, light-colored igneous rock.

MAGMA—molten rock materials.

MATRIX—the natural rock material in which is imbedded any large crystals, fossils, or rock fragments.

MELTWATER—water resulting from the melting of snow or glacial ice.

METAMORPHISM—the process by which consolidated rocks are altered in composition, texture, or internal structure by high temperatures and pressures within the earth.

METASEDIMENTARY ROCK—a sedimentary rock which has undergone heat and pressure.

MICA—a silicate mineral which easily breaks into thin sheets.

MINERAL—a naturally occurring element or compound with a definite range of chemical composition and usually a characteristic crystal form.

MINERALOGY—the mineral composition of a rock.

MINERAL SUITE—the array of minerals within a body of rock.

MONZONITE—a medium- to coarse-grained intrusive igneous rock containing approximately equal amounts of orthoclase and plagioclase. Quartz is usually present.

MORAINE—an irregular accumulation of glacial drift having constructional topography. There are many kinds of moraines—end moraines or terminal moraines, ground moraines, and moraine complexes.

MUD CRACKS—cracks formed in mud by desiccation.

MUSKEG—a northern, poorly drained, flat-lying landscape. Moss, heath, tamarack, and spruce grow here.

OLIVINE—a common rock-forming, green-colored, magnesium and iron silicate.

ORTHOCLASE—a silicate mineral of the feldspar group. Orthoclase is often pink to white in color, has a chemical composition of $KAlSi_3O_8$, and is a common mineral in granitic rocks.

OUTCROP—any rock exposure.

OUTWASH—the stratified sands and gravels laid down by meltwater streams.

PALEONTOLOGIST—one who studies the life of the past through fossils.

PEAT—partially decomposed plant material often found in swamps.

PERMAFROST—perennially frozen ground.

PHYSIOGRAPHIC—refers to landforms.

PHYSIOGRAPHY—the study of the genesis and evolution of landforms.

PLAGIOCLASE—a sodium-calcium mineral series within the feldspar group.

PORPHYRITIC—a textural term used for igneous rocks in which larger crystals are set in a matrix of finer crystals.

POTHOLE—a rounded hole, deeper than it is wide, formed in solid rock. Potholes are generally formed on stream bottoms, at the base of falls, or in strong rapids, where sand and gravel have been spun around by the force of the current and cut into the stream floor.

QUARTZ—an extremely common silicate mineral with a chemical composition of SiO_2. Quartz comes in many colors and named varieties, including agate, amethyst, and chalcedony.

QUARTZITE—a granular metamorphic rock consisting essentially of quartz; also any sandstone firmly cemented by silica.

RADIOCARBON—a radioactive isotope of carbon; ^{14}C.

RELIEF—the difference in elevation between the high and the low points on the land surface. High relief indicates that there is a considerable difference; low relief that there is little difference.

RHYOLITE—a fine-grained igneous rock of the same composition as granite.

RIFT—a continent-sized fault.

ROCHE MOUTONNÉES—"sheep back" rock. This is a French word denoting a glacially striated and rounded bedrock hill.

ROCK—a naturally occurring aggregate of minerals, or single mineral mass

SANDPLAIN—level countryside underlain by outwash sand.

SANDSPIT—a narrow sand point.

SANDSTONE—a consolidated rock composed of sand grains.

SCARP—an escarpment, cliff.

SCOUR—erosion, especially by moving water or glacial ice.

SEDGE—a plant which resembles grass but has hollow rather than solid stems.

SEDIMENT—the solid material, either mineral or organic, that is in suspension and being transported by air, water, or ice; also that same material when it has settled from suspension.

SEDIMENTARY ROCK—rocks formed from sediments, especially clastic rocks formed from fragments of older rocks, but also rocks formed by precipitation of chemical substances from solution or from the secretions of organisms.

SEQUENCE—a succession.

SHALE—sedimentary rock formed from clay particles.

SHIELD—a regional, dome-shaped mass of exposed Precambrian rock.

SILICATE—a mineral containing silicon-oxygen tetrahedra.

SILICON—an element which occurs extensively in the earth's crust, atomic number 14, atomic weight 28.086.

SILL—a tabular-shaped body of intrusive igneous rock which has been emplaced parallel to the structure of the surrounding rock.

SILT—a clastic sediment with particles midway in size between those of clay and sand.

222   *Glossary*

SILTSTONE—consolidated silt.

SINK, SINKHOLE—a funnel-shaped hole formed on the earth's surface through the dissolution of limestone.

SLATE—a fine-grained, generally dark-colored metamorphic rock which breaks along flat planes.

SPHAGNUM—a type of large moss. This is a common name and also a genus name.

SPHENE—a silicate mineral containing calcium and titanium.

STALACTITE—a cylindrical mineral deposit, generally calcite, hanging from the roof of a cave.

STALAGMITE—a conical mineral deposit, generally calcite, arising from the floor of a cave.

STRANDLINE—a beach.

STRATIGRAPHIC SEQUENCE—the chronologically arranged succession of sedimentary rocks. The older rocks are at the bottom and the younger rocks are at the top.

STRATIGRAPHY—a branch of geology which considers the formation, composition, sequence, and correlation of layered rocks.

STRIATIONS—scratches on a rock surface, generally caused by overriding glacial ice.

STRIKE-SLIP FAULT—a fault with primary movement along the strike of the fault.

SUBAQUEOUS—underwater.

SURFICIAL, SURFICIAL MATERIAL—soil, clay, silt, sand, gravel. The unconsolidated, or loose, rock materials on the surface of the earth. *Surficial material* is used in contrast to *bedrock*.

SWELL AND SWALE—a type of low-relief landscape characterized by domelike hills and slight marshy depressions.

TACONITE—an iron-bearing chert. Taconite is the predominant rock of Minnesota's iron ranges.

TERRACE—a bench, or relatively flat, long, narrow surface within the landscape. Steeper slopes occur on each side of the bench.

TERRAIN—a tract of land, considered as to its topography.

TERRANE—the surface over which a particular rock or group of rocks is exposed.

TILL, GLACIAL TILL—the nonsorted rock materials deposited directly by a glacier.

TILL PLAIN—a subdued landscape of glacial drift.

TOMBOLO—a rock or sand point connecting an island with the mainland or another island.

TONALITE—a medium-grained igneous rock containing both light and dark minerals, including quartz.

TOPOGRAPHIC MAP—a map showing the configuration of the land surface by means of contour lines, lines connecting points of equal elevation.

TOPOGRAPHY—the study of the land surface, especially the physical features of a district and the contour of the land; also the configuration of the land.

TRILOBITE—a three-lobed arthropod which lived in Paleozoic seas.

TUFF—a rock formed of small compacted volcanic fragments.

UNDERFIT STREAM—a stream appearing too small for its valley.

UPLIFT—elevation of part of the earth's surface.

URALITE—a variety of hornblende occurring in altered rock.

VESICLE—any gas cavity within an igneous rock.

VOLCANIC—pertaining to volcanoes.

WATER TABLE—the upper surface of the zone of water saturation within the earth.

WEATHER—to undergo change because of exposure to the atmosphere.

WEATHERING—a group of processes,

physical and chemical, which cause the breakdown of rock.

WETLAND—a lowland area saturated with moisture, such as a marsh or swamp.

ZIRCON—a dull, colorless mineral: $ZrSiO_4$.